W9-ATC-919

"Mark Sanborn has done it again. Regardless of what department you work in or what your job description says, *Fred 2.0* demonstrates you can provide greater service, build better relationships, and create more value. It is not just a recipe for finding more satisfaction at work; it's a blueprint for fixing our global economy."

MICHAEL HYATT
New York Times bestselling author and former CEO of
Thomas Nelson Publishers

"At Zappos we have been using *The Fred Factor* for several years to inspire our employees to take ownership of customer service and to use their own experiences to live and deliver *wow*."

TONY HSIEH
CEO of Zappos.com Inc. and *New York Times* bestselling author of
Delivering Happiness

"I promise that if you take Mark Sanborn's advice to heart and begin a more 'Fred-like' existence, you will never view yourself the same way again."

JOHN C. MAXWELL
Popular speaker and bestselling author of *The 21 Irrefutable Laws of Leadership*

"In *Fred 2.0* Mark Sanborn shares extraordinary examples of people who are committed to service. This book encourages us as individuals and companies to live with intent, passion, and integrity as our guiding principles. *Fred 2.0* is a book everyone in a service business will want to read and share!"

JENNIFER M. GRIFFITH
President of Commerce National Bank

Fred 2.0

★

Fred

2.0

NEW IDEAS ON HOW TO KEEP DELIVERING EXTRAORDINARY RESULTS

MARK SANBORN

Tyndale House Publishers, Inc.
Carol Stream, Illinois

Visit Tyndale online at www.tyndale.com.

Visit Mark Sanborn's website at www.marksanborn.com.

TYNDALE and Tyndale's quill logo are registered trademarks of Tyndale House Publishers, Inc.

Fred 2.0: New Ideas on How to Keep Delivering Extraordinary Results

Designed by Mark Anthony Lane II

Edited by Stephanie Rische

Published in association with Yates & Yates (www.yates2.com).

Library of Congress Cataloging-in-Publication Data

Sanborn, Mark.
  Fred 2.0 : new ideas on how to keep delivering extraordinary results / Mark Sanborn.
    p. cm.
  ISBN 978-1-4143-6220-5
  1. Success—Religious aspects—Christianity. I. Title.
  BV4598.3.S26 2013
  158—dc23   2012040337

Printed in the United States of America

19   18   17   16   15
7

To Fred Shea, the real deal and a valued friend.

Thank you for your example.

Contents

Foreword

I FIRST LEARNED about the real-life mailman Fred Shea several years ago when Mark Sanborn spoke at a conference I was attending. The principles Mark taught that day—that everybody can make a difference, that relationships are vital, that it's possible to add value in every area, that you can keep reinventing yourself—have the power to change lives and corporate cultures.

These principles resonated with me because they're woven into my organization, the worldwide RE/MAX network of nearly ninety thousand real estate agents. We simply wouldn't be where we are today without many of the core values Mark communicates so well. I remember returning to the office and sharing his "Fred principles" with my leadership team. They were impressed.

A big takeaway from Mark's work is that it's not enough to know how to be a Fred; you have to take action on that understanding. Put what you know to work for you, and you have all you need to create customers for life.

Fred 2.0 is a fascinating step forward for the concept. Read it and you'll understand how to keep the energy of Fred alive and well in your organization, year after year. The book serves as an advanced course in how to go beyond the ordinary to create extraordinary experiences for your clients, no matter what type of business you're in. It also teaches you to dig deeper within to change your attitude and outlook so you can share the Fred message with others.

Fred 2.0 explains how maintaining a creative focus on service can drive the results you're seeking. I think the lessons in this book will truly benefit readers, whether they work on their own or lead massive organizations. It's all here—it's just a matter of absorbing the message and putting it into practice every day.

Mark's Fred principles are insightful, practical, and motivational—and they can do amazing things for your career and your life. In the end, Mark is absolutely correct in saying that business relies on relationships. So when you focus on creating winning results for people—whether they're clients, colleagues, friends, or even strangers—you open yourself up to a world of possibilities and a life of success.

Margaret Kelly, CEO of RE/MAX

Introduction

Why Fred 2.0?

I'm in one of America's busiest airports, milling around with dozens of other travelers. Due to some extreme weather conditions, all of us are anxiously awaiting an update on our plane's departure—or lack thereof.

This is not an unusual place for me to be, since I travel for a living—or at least it feels that way sometimes. I used to work in sales and marketing, and now I'm in the idea business—speaking, writing, and advising leaders. So in the past thirty years I have gained a certain intimacy with the hospitality industry in general and with airlines, airports, and hotels in particular.

Today I notice that, despite the anxiety of passengers, the airline personnel show little concern—with one notable exception. The lone gate agent.

While the other airline employees who have come and gone for the past two hours of the weather delay seem nonplussed by the passengers' angst, the gate agent has shown genuine concern and empathy. She has been hustling to get as much information as possible from her various sources.

She is also the object of misplaced aggression. She isn't

personally responsible for the weather, but you'd never know that from the carping of some of the passengers. We listen to her latest announcement.

"I apologize that I can't give you more information," she offers sincerely. "If there were anything more I could do, I would. Right now I'm waiting to hear from our pilots if and when the flight will be departing. I will provide an update every ten minutes, even if the best I can offer is 'I still don't know.'"

The four basic Fred principles:

1. **Everybody makes a difference.**
2. **It is all built on relationship.**
3. **You can add value to everything you do.**
4. **You can reinvent yourself continually.**

The man next to me is wearing a sport coat without a tie. He says, almost to himself, "I just wish there were more Freds like her at this airline."

Freds?

"Excuse me," I say, "but you just said something about the gate agent being a *Fred*. What did you mean by that?"

"Oh, it's a phrase we use at our company for someone who does a great job regardless of their circumstances. We got the idea from a book we studied a few years ago. It's called *The Fred Factor*, and it's about an amazing postal carrier in Denver."[1]

"I'm familiar with the book." I smile. "I wrote it."

"No kidding? Hey, great to meet you!" He reaches out to shake my hand. "Your book raised our awareness about how each of us could deliver more value and be of greater service to

---

[1] If you would like to know the story of the real-life Fred the Postman, you can download a free copy of *The Fred Factor* story at http://www.marksanborn.com/fredfactorstory.

each other and to our customers. We even give out a monthly Fred award."

After a pause, he continues, "But I'm just wondering, what ever happened to Fred? Do you have any plans to write a follow-up book?"

I've been asked that question (or a variation on it) dozens of times since *The Fred Factor* was released. I've received e-mails, phone calls, letters, and packages from individuals, organizations, and schools that have embraced the Fred philosophy. Every time I hear from someone who has been positively impacted by the message of Fred the Postman through my books and speeches, I'm gratified. But what is an author to do with those lingering follow-up questions?

The way I see it, if you get asked the same questions enough times, you should answer them.

How's Fred doing now?

What can I do to keep delivering extraordinary results?

What are some new ways I can apply these principles in my work and life?

Good questions. I will answer them in the pages ahead.

Mark Sanborn

CHAPTER I

NORMAL IS OVERRATED

*We all carry the seeds of greatness within us, but we need an
image as a point of focus in order that they may sprout.*
EPICTETUS

THE FRED CONCEPT is based on the story of the real-life postal
carrier Fred Shea, who delivered my mail for nearly a decade.
When I first met Fred, I was so impressed by his performance
that I started paying attention, taking notes about him and
talking about him in my speeches and seminars, and ultimately
writing a book about him. The account of his ability to take the
ordinary job of putting mail in a box day after day and make
it extraordinary made a connection with those who heard or
read it.

It's hard to believe that a simple story about a mailman took
off the way it did, but since *The Fred Factor* was released in
2004, it went on to become the number six bestselling business
book of the year, according to *Businessweek* magazine. Since
that time it has sold more than 1.6 million copies in the United
States and around the world.

I share that because it is gratifying to know that someone

who does an ordinary job in an extraordinary way can have such a powerful impact on people around the world.

Don't settle for normal. Choose to be extraordinary.

Why did the book succeed? I think a main reason is because it wasn't about a big name like Bill Gates or Warren Buffett. When we read about such titans of business success, we tend to think, *Well, yeah, they're geniuses. I'm just an ordinary person working at a normal job. They're among the richest people on the planet!*

What does Fred have to work with? He has a blue-gray uniform and a bag. That's pretty much it once he leaves the substation. And yet he makes artistry out of his work.

If Fred can be extraordinary in what could be a tedious job, then there is no reason why you and I can't reinvent our own work, whatever it may be.

MAILMAN MIKE'S STORY

We all love a good story, and the best stories are true.

So let me tell you a story about another incredible mail carrier. He is beloved by the people on his route for his cheerfulness, his encouragement, and his love for both his work and his customers. He consistently goes beyond the call of duty and has become such an important part of his customers' lives that they tell others about the incredible work he does. His commitment to his job and his community has even gotten him media attention.

He's Mailman Mike, from West Covina, California.

I learned about Mike from Angela Carter, who contacted me after reading *The Fred Factor*.

"After reading your book," she wrote, "I thought to myself, *He just has to hear about our mailman. . . .*"

Mike's name is Michael Flowers, but on his route he's better known by the name Brother Love. He's committed to his wife and three children—and also to the people he delivers mail to.

Angela related the story of when she first met Mailman Mike. She was going through a difficult period in her life and was dealing with deep sadness. As she was going into her house, Mike yelled out from across the street, "Hi, beautiful!" His simple encouragement was music to her ears.

From that point on, she began talking to Mike each day when he delivered her mail. She also discovered how much Mike meant to the other people on the route. Angela sent me pictures and notes to illustrate her point.

Mike, Angela says, knows everyone on his route by name, along with some of the circumstances they are facing. She has no idea how he can remember so much about those he serves.

For instance, each year Mike deep-fries turkeys for people on his route and gives them as Thanksgiving and Christmas gifts. (If he misses someone on Thanksgiving, he makes sure they get a turkey at Christmas.) When he was featured in the local newspaper, some of his customers had the article framed and presented it to him.

On Mother's Day, Mike brought Angela flowers.

"I call Mrs. Carter *Mom*," Mike said. "There are several people in my life I give that name to. It's a title I do not take lightly. I feel the people who inspire me deserve a better salutation from me than just *Mrs.* What's even better is that they allow me to call them *Mom.* How sweet is that?"

But then came trouble. The postal service reorganized

routes, and Mike was assigned a new area. His customers were distraught. They asked if they could get him back, but they were told flatly that it wasn't possible.

The Bible says, "With God all things are possible." With customers who are raving fans, many things are possible too.

Thanks to guidance from the newspaper editor who wrote the article about Mike, this neighborhood mounted a campaign, starting with their congresswoman. Then Angela went door-to-door with a petition. She was amazed at the response.

"I couldn't believe how Mike was so humble, yet his life had touched so many."

The group's persistence paid off. One hundred days after Mike was taken off the route, he was reassigned to his old territory.

With her letter, Angela included a picture of her street, taken the day Mike returned. Neighbors had tied yellow ribbons to every tree and bush to welcome him back.

The newspaper article includes this quote by Michael Flowers, aka Brother Love: "If God didn't give me anything else, he gave me love."

FREDS AND MIKES ARE EVERYWHERE

In the years since *The Fred Factor* came out, I've received hundreds of similar stories about Freds—individuals who turn the ordinary into the extraordinary. These people are diverse in their jobs, backgrounds, and life experiences. In addition to stories about postal carriers, I've heard numerous accounts of customer service professionals who went above and beyond the call of duty. But Freds also showed up in unexpected places. Some educators adopted the principles in their schools, businesses implemented company-wide Fred initiatives, and a prison instituted a program for inmates using *The Fred Factor*. A city was even declared Fredville, USA. (You'll read many of these stories and examples in the pages ahead.)

What makes these stories fascinating is that they stand in stark contrast to indifferent employees, unhelpful coworkers, and rude experiences—what we often think of as "normal." When we run into a Fred, we are pleasantly surprised, if not outright delighted.

Frankly, if the anecdotes and stories were normal and unremarkable, I wouldn't be writing about them because you wouldn't be interested in reading them.

The common trait that all these individuals share? None of them settled for normal, average, or ordinary. They all chose to be better than normal; they chose to be extraordinary.

WHY BE NORMAL?

We don't talk much about normal unless we want to get back to it after a period of upheaval. That's because normal is what we get used to. Normal is easy, familiar. But is that the best we can aim for each day—to be normal?

Peggy Noonan, one of my favorite writers, recently commented that people who run for president often try to come across as normal. In her column, she points out that wanting to be the leader of the free world really isn't normal, and it isn't something most people aspire to or are capable of. But she doesn't see it as a bad thing that they're different from the average person. "Anyway," she says, "normal is overrated."

I love to ski, and being from Colorado, I get many opportunities to do so. When I meet people on ski lifts, they tell me they love the mountain experience and are sad when they have to head home to normal. I hear a similar sentiment when I'm vacationing at the beach. Even after people are congratulated on receiving an award, they sometimes talk about how they'll feel when things are back to normal.

If you want more out of life, go for more. Raise your expectations. Settle up, rather than down.

Is it possible that we aim too low? Maybe the thrill of the ski run, the relaxation of the beach, or the exhilaration of an award should be our benchmark for normal rather than the monotony of everyday life.

No one can live on the mountaintop all the time. And it is often said that valleys help us appreciate the high points in life. But while that may be true, too many people seem to accept the valley as a permanent residence.

I like to *aspire higher*. If you want more out of life, go for more. Raise your expectations. Settle up, rather than down.

In other words, *recalibrate to great*.

PURSUE EXTRAORDINARY

"Nobody can prevent you from choosing to be extraordinary."

In 2004, management guru Tom Peters chose this quote from *The Fred Factor* as one of his favorites of the year. The statement is simple but true. Whether you are encouraged, taught, rewarded, or recognized for being extraordinary, at the end of the day it is a choice *you* have to make. No one else can make it for you—not your employer, not your spouse, not your friend. It's something you have to pursue yourself.

The Benefits of Extraordinary

So what's the point of exerting extra thought and effort into being extraordinary?

You will receive many benefits from being extraordinary. But after studying extraordinary individuals and organizations for more than twenty-five years, I've identified four of the most powerful benefits.

1. **Extraordinary brings us delight.** Just as a spectacular sunrise has the ability to jump-start our senses and remind us of the wonders of life, an extraordinary act or experience, whether we provide it or experience it, increases our joy. That is why stories of the extraordinary go viral. They are not just unusual—they are inspirational. We want to share the delight with others.

2. **Extraordinary sets us apart.** Goethe said there are so many echoes and so few voices. Many resources, it seems, are undifferentiated commodities that we could get from anyone, anywhere, anytime. Employees who offer nothing different from other employees are interchangeable—and they likely won't go far in their careers.

   If everything we provide, as individuals or organizations, is exactly the same as what others provide, there is no reason for customers to choose us, our products, or our services above others. That means the competition always will be based on price—lowest price, to be exact. If we want to be in demand as an employee or employer, or as a product or service provider, we need to make sure we offer customers the ultimate differentiator: an extraordinary experience.

3. **Extraordinary defends our position.** The price for sloppiness and mediocrity is higher today than it ever has been. If consumers can get better service or value elsewhere, they'll abandon the inferior for the superior without giving a second thought to loyalty. It is difficult and expensive to get customers, land a job, and form new relationships. If we aren't committed to continually delighting the important people in our businesses (and in our lives), we run the risk that they'll go elsewhere. Our best defense is when someone says, "There is nobody like him or her. I won't accept a substitute."

4. **Extraordinary determines our happiness and success.** A life well lived is the sum of extraordinary effort, extraordinary relationships, and extraordinary results. There's nothing wrong with ordinary if that's all we aspire to. The problem, as I see it, is that many people would like to be extraordinary but fear disappointment, so they settle. Normal becomes enough—not because it is desirable, but because it is a safer alternative to the pursuit of the extraordinary.

Pastor and author Bill Hybels says, "Personally, I've never understood inactivity. Why a person would sit when he could soar, spectate when he could play, or atrophy when he could develop is beyond me."

The good news is that the difference between ordinary and extraordinary isn't as big as you might think.

Alecia Is Extraordinary

My family enjoys eating at a Mexican restaurant in our neighborhood. One night my wife, Darla, wasn't feeling well and asked the boys and me to bring back an order for her when we finished dining.

The three of us loaded up and drove to the restaurant. When our waitress, Alecia, came to take our order, I said, "My wife is under the weather, so I'm going to order her food now. If you'll just try to time it so it's ready to go when we're finished, I'd be grateful."

Alecia was attentive and cheerful as she served us that evening. At the end of our meal, she brought out a bag with two Styrofoam containers of food for Darla. On one she'd written in red ink, "Hope you're feeling better. {Smiley face.} Alecia."

When we got home, Darla asked, "Who's Alecia?"

After I explained, she was touched by Alecia's thoughtfulness.

The next time we ate at that restaurant, we asked if we could be seated in Alecia's section. Again, she did an extraordinary job.

A few weeks later when we returned, we asked if Alecia was working.

"She is, but her section is full," the hostess informed us.

"That's fine," we said. "We'll wait."

Alecia wasn't a manager. She didn't have any special privileges. And she certainly didn't have a company budget. Yet with just a tiny bit of extra effort and a red pen, she took her service from ordinary to extraordinary.

We all have that same opportunity to go beyond the typical, beyond what is normal or expected. If we choose, we can do things—large and small—that enrich the lives of those we live and work with, as well as our own lives.

After all, normal is overrated.

....

THE FRED CHECKLIST

☐ Goes beyond what is expected

☐ Isn't content with being "normal"

☐ Does ordinary things in an extraordinary way

☐ Loves his/her job

☐ Cares about the people he/she works with and for

CHAPTER 2

WHAT EVER HAPPENED TO FRED?

It's time to start living the life you've imagined.
HENRY JAMES

THE MOST COMMONLY asked question I get about Fred is, "Does Fred really exist?"

When I speak about him or when people read about him in *The Fred Factor*, the most common response is inspiration ("Wow, that's amazing!"). But it's not uncommon for other people to react in disbelief ("Come on, you're making that up!").

Some people wonder if I've invented him, if he's a composite of different individuals, or if he's an imaginary character based on a set of virtues.

I've gotten used to the skepticism. We are all familiar with what is called "literary license." Authors and speakers tend to embellish their stories to make them more dramatic or entertaining. I understand that, and in certain cases in my own writing and speaking, I have had to change the details of a particular story (but not the core elements) to protect someone's privacy.

But I haven't embellished or changed the story of Fred the Postman, the real-life Fred Shea. I've retold the details as accurately as I can from my personal interactions with Fred and our exchanges over the years.

Fred himself confirms this: "The way you've written it is the way it is. That is how I live my life. Nothing in *The Fred Factor* is fiction."

Sometimes you just can't improve on the truth. Having known Fred now for more than twenty years, I can tell you that in real life he is indeed the same person he is in the story I've told.

After reading *The Fred Factor*, someone told me that I didn't share enough information about Fred or develop him as a "character." There are several reasons for that approach. First, he's not a character; he's a person—and my friend. Second, I wanted to be respectful of him and his privacy. I shared what I felt was important to the story and what Fred would be comfortable with having me share.

WHERE IS FRED TODAY?

Over the years my wife, Darla, and I have stayed in touch with Fred and his wife, Kathie. Our schedules don't allow us to get together as much as we'd like, but we meet periodically for dinner and have kept in touch through cards, e-mails, and phone calls.

Recently I invited Fred to lunch to get an update on him, his work, and what has happened since *The Fred Factor* was published.

Fred is no longer working in Washington Park, Colorado, where he worked when I first met him. Today he is delivering mail to about a thousand apartments in the Cherry Creek area, not too far from his old route.

One of the things that has always amazed me is how little

recognition Fred has received for his work. At the time the book was released, Fred had been doing an extraordinary job for the USPS for more than twenty years, yet he never received any formal recognition. Fred's customers and coworkers knew he did an exceptional job, but his efforts went largely unnoticed by management. His station did hold a nice ceremony for him when the book was released, but that was about the extent of his accolades.

Fred isn't bitter or unhappy. He does what he does for his own reasons—not to get ahead, to get recognized, or to move up in the organization. He is realistic in his appraisal not just of his employer but also of organizations in general: "The problem at work is that they forget about you because you're not a troublemaker."

It's ironic, isn't it, how poor performance tends to get more attention than good performance? We effectively feed our problems and starve our star performers.

THE INFLUENCES IN FRED'S LIFE

You might guess that Fred is exceptional because he was the product of great parenting, but you'd be wrong.

Fred was the youngest of three kids. By his own account, his parents weren't kind or affectionate but self-absorbed. It's tough for Fred to discuss, but he's honest about it.

"I prayed I'd never be like my parents," he told me over lunch.

As sad as that is, Fred is proof that parenting—good *or* bad—traps nobody. As adults, we make our own choices. And Fred chose to be of greater service to others not *because of* but *in spite of* how he was raised.

Music has always been an important part of Fred's life. "I played music for twenty years," Fred told me. "I started with the drums at the age of eight, and that was my life. When I was a kid, if I wasn't in school or at work, I was practicing. I always enjoyed it. I tended not to like crowds, but the one exception was when I was playing the drums. Then it was different—the bigger the crowd, the better I played."

Fred's love for music wasn't something he kept to himself when he became an adult.

"I refinished drums for kids who couldn't afford them," he said. "My parents would never buy me a good set of drums when I was young, so I liked helping kids who wanted to play by giving them what I never had."

Another constant in Fred's life has been his strong work ethic. "I worked even when I was in grade school," he said. "I delivered papers, sold peanut brittle, and picked up cans in the alley to turn in for cash. I did whatever it took to provide for myself."

That sense of purpose has carried over into adulthood—both to his professional life and to his personal life. "I have a hard time sitting through an entire movie because there are always things that need to be done, things I want to be doing."

THE MILLION-DOLLAR QUESTION

People who have heard me speak about Fred often ask the same question: Why does he do it? After all, he doesn't get paid more for going beyond what is expected.

I had known Fred for at least a decade before I directly asked him why he does what he does. As I was looking over the manuscript one more time just prior to publication, I decided to include a chapter about what motivates Fred (it became chapter 12: "Fred Today"). I discovered that, in essence, the reason Fred does what he does is so old-fashioned and basic it may surprise you. Fred does what he does because he knows it's the right thing to do.

He can't quite understand why this approach to work and life seems so, well, unusual today. He isn't sure why everyone else doesn't think and act the same way.

I asked Fred what keeps him going at age sixty-three, almost a decade after *The Fred Factor* was released. He responded, "The same things that kept me going before the book came out."

He reflected for a moment. "I like doing things for people because it makes me feel better. I know I've done a good job if I take care of my customers—although I don't think of them as customers; I think of them as my friends or the folks on my route. Some people might not even have a clue what I've done for them, but that's okay. I don't do it so they'll know— I do it because it's the right thing to do."

> **Fred does what he does because he knows it's the right thing to do.**

Fred smiled. "I've got less hair and fewer teeth now," he said, "but I don't have less heart."

WHO ARE FRED'S FREDS?

When I asked Fred about the people in his own life who have inspired him, he didn't hesitate.

"My wife, Kathie," he said. "She's the best Fred I've ever met. We've been married for more than forty years, and I love her more today than the day I met her. I feel I've done a few good things in my life, like marrying Kathie and raising our boys. Now my joy is my two grandbabies."

Fred is traditional in his beliefs and refreshingly old-fashioned. He shared this story about his younger days: "I courted Kathie for four years and eight months before we got married. We lived about twenty miles apart, and in all that time there was never a month that I didn't see her. We didn't live together. I courted her."

"Will your grandkids become Freds?" I inquired.

"It's a good possibility. Kathie and I spend lots of time with them. We built a play center in our backyard, we take them to the park, and we've gotten them bicycles. But best of all, they've learned to have real love and real respect for everyone."

"MRS. FRED"

If success is being respected and loved most by those who know you best, then Fred Shea has achieved it. His wife, Kathie, and sons, Bryan and Justin, are his biggest fans. I know this to be true based on the time I've spent with them—by the things they've said and the affection they've shown.

After I interviewed Fred to get an update on his life, my wife, Darla, wisely suggested I interview Kathie.

When I called her, she was recovering from a knee replacement, so she had time to talk—and a story to tell.

"Fred has been so helpful as I recover from this painful surgery. The doctors suggested that I change positions frequently, and at night I wake up about every ninety minutes when my leg starts throbbing. Fred gets up to help me change the position of my knee, which I would have a hard time doing without him. When I go to bed, he tucks me in, situates my pillow, and makes sure

I have everything I need. I joke with him and say, 'I'll see you in an hour and a half!' And of course I do. But he never complains."

It quickly became clear that Kathie was only getting started. "I've had to kick him out of the house to go get coffee or have breakfast with Justin. He doesn't want to leave me, but I make sure he gets a break when my sisters come to help. Even then, he is reluctant. Before the surgery he installed a new flexible shower-head and got a special chair for the shower. He did everything he could to make sure I had a good recovery."

I can't think of anything that would serve as better proof that Fred lives a life of service to others, whether at home or at work.

"Fred is a very humble person," Kathie shared. "He wouldn't tell anybody about *The Fred Factor* book or bring attention to himself, but if you have questions for him, he'll share anything you want to know. He doesn't go for his own recognition, but he's always happy to help out however he can."

"Fred is who the book portrays him to be," she confirmed. "Even after forty-three years of marriage, I'm still amazed how much generosity he has in his heart."

Kathie knows that Fred has become who he is in spite of a tough childhood and parents who weren't supportive. "He had to turn his life around, and he did it from within. It has made him a better person by 150 percent."

Fred's son Justin is one of Fred's most loyal fans. He told me he wants to be the type of man that his father is.

"When Dad comes home, he has a routine—he's always been this way. He doesn't come home and relax. He stays busy all the time."

"In the end," his son said, "the book hasn't changed him. Fred is still Fred."

WHAT'S NEXT FOR FRED?

I know how much Fred Shea has positively influenced me, and I have a sense of the ways his example has touched other people worldwide. But I was curious: How had the book impacted him?

"It is the single most overwhelming thing that has impacted me personally. Getting married had a big effect on both Kathie and me, as did having our kids. But aside from those events, this has had the biggest impact on me personally."

A thoughtful look came across Fred's face. "I never dreamed the book would be so big and still going after all these years," he said. "I never felt like I deserved it. People think I had a lot to do with it, but *you* wrote the story. I do get recognized sometimes. A guy who knew me once yelled across a store, 'Hey, isn't that Fred the Postman?'"

Fred still works full time for the USPS. He loves his wife and sons, and he dotes on his grandbabies. He keeps busy doing the things he feels need to be done. So what's next for him?

"Retire?" Fred sounded surprised at the suggestion. "I don't know. . . . I only think about that when somebody else brings it up."

In my book *Up, Down, or Sideways,* I wrote that faith, family, and friends are—for me—the essential blessings of life. The cake, if you will. The rest is icing.

I haven't heard Fred put it in exactly those words, but I've seen him live that way. I think that's one reason why we respect and appreciate each other so much. Fred has shared with me about his faith in God and his deep appreciation for what we both feel are God's greatest blessings in our lives—family and friends.

In this age of fame and celebrity, Fred is taking a different path. He's appreciative of the recognition he has received, but he isn't doing anything differently now that he has been the central figure in a bestselling book.

He still loves his family, his coworkers, his customers, and his work. He is a man of quiet faith. And when it comes down to it, that's all that truly matters to him.

Take life one day at a time, and make each day better than the last.

As we finished lunch, Fred offered this final suggestion: "Take life one day at a time, and make each day better than the last."

SELF-REFLECTION

1. Who and what have been the consistent influences in your life? How have they influenced you?

2. Whom do you most want to influence? How are you doing that?

3. Consider this life-purpose question: Why do you do what you do?

4. Who are the Freds in your life? (Why not let them know how much you appreciate their influence?)

CHAPTER 3

IT'S ALWAYS
ABOUT SERVICE

What we do for a living does not matter as much as how we do it.
ORISON SWETT MARDEN

BUSINESS CONSULTANT David Goldsmith teaches individual and organizational performance. He tells the story about an American company that had worked for years negotiating a deal to sell laser equipment to a prospective buyer in Japan. As a final step in the negotiations, they were to ship one of the lasers to Japan for a thorough inspection. If it met the Japanese buyer's strict quality standards—standards that surpassed those of the US domestic market—the American company would close its sale.

When the equipment arrived, it was thoroughly tested and inspected. The laser passed with flying colors, and the sale seemed imminent. But then one of the buyer's managers caught a glimpse of something in the laser's packaging that didn't look quite right.

When he glanced into the shipping carton, he found a shoe

print left behind by one of the packagers at the American facility. Since the footprint was on the inside of the box—a surface never exposed during the manufacturing process—the manager could only conclude that the footprint had been caused by the American manufacturer's sloppiness.

The manager directed his team to repackage the laser into its box, along with the following message: "If you can manage to get a footprint in the box, I can't imagine what you might have done to the product."

The company had to put in another two years of grueling effort, not to mention money, to restore confidence and ultimately complete the sale. A sale that was nearly lost because someone in shipping obviously wasn't a Fred.

Fred doesn't always work in the customer service department. But he (or she) is always about service.

IS FRED THE ONLY FACTOR?

Based on feedback I've received from readers and organizations that use *The Fred Factor*, I know that many people have applied the principles in customer service contexts. I'm delighted that the book has found a niche there, but the truth is that I didn't set out to write about customer service. My intent was to write a simple book of business philosophy.

Philosophy answers the question, how should we live? A business philosophy book addresses how we should do business.

To me, Fred Shea exemplifies the principles I've seen in most successful individuals and organizations that make a positive difference.

These principles are about more than business—they

are about life. Some people grasp these concepts intuitively, and others manage to learn them along the way. But it's rare that they specifically are taught. I often hear managers implore employees to "create value" and "build better relationships," but they rarely offer training programs to teach them how.

What is a *factor*? It's defined as one of the elements that contributes to a particular result or situation. A factor isn't the only element, or even the most important element. It is simply part of the mix. Being extraordinary in whatever you do is a key element to achieving success—or more of it. But it isn't enough on its own. Doing something above the call of duty for a customer won't take you very far if your product is inferior or if your price is outrageous or if everyone else on your team negates your best efforts with their indifference.

There are no singular solutions. Be wary of any author, speaker, or expert who claims that he or she has a single-bullet approach that will cover it all. That said, the Fred philosophy can be a factor in literally every aspect of your business—and your life. It applies as much to the time you spend with family and friends and your involvement in your community as it does to what you do each day at work and your interactions with customers and clients.

The Fred philosophy is built on timeless values like personal responsibility, authentic relationships, and respect for others. It is, in essence, a mind-set that looks for and seizes opportunities to turn the ordinary into the extraordinary.

Even so, it's one thing to know and another thing to do. Intentions don't count for much without actions. Being a Fred is about what we believe *and* what we do.

THE WHY IS ALWAYS A WHO

On one of my many airline travels, I was sitting next to a fellow inconvenienced traveler. We had just gotten word of our second mechanical delay, and the gate agent was trying to determine if the flight would be further delayed, canceled, or shifted to another plane.

My new friend muttered, "Well, you can't really blame anyone for the delay. After all, it was a mechanical problem."

Au contraire. I wasn't trying to place blame, I explained, but people were responsible for every aspect of the delay: the maintenance people, who might have spotted the problem before the plane was scheduled to depart; the ground crew, who could have quickly diagnosed the problem; or the operations people, who could have found an available alternative flight for us.

Sure, mechanical delays are hard to control, but the deepest impressions on every flier were most definitely formed by *who* problems, not *what* problems. The reasons we like or dislike, enjoy or suffer, stay or go away stem from a who.

Why do you do business with a certain company? Great prices? A person was responsible for the pricing. Wonderful service? Obviously people provide that. High-quality products? Thank the people in research, development, and manufacturing.

IS IT ENOUGH TO ARRIVE ALIVE?

After another particularly trying experience on a well-known airline (and we all have so many airline injustice stories, it wouldn't do any good for me to point fingers here), I wrote a blog post addressed to the airline's management. My social media team told me the blog had approximately three hundred thousand impressions, which served as a striking reminder that word of mouth can hurt your business, but word of *mouse* can really sink your boat.

Word of mouth can hurt your business, but word of *mouse* can really sink your boat.

I received hundreds of comments about the post. One said, "Hey, quit complaining. After all, you eventually got to your destination safely, and that is what flying is all about." It would be hard to argue against arriving safely. It's true—that is the first consideration of flying. But it's not the only one. Great service certainly won't mitigate an air disaster. But if arriving safely were the only issue, then a good motto for the airline I flew would have been, "At least you didn't die." Maybe it's a lot to ask, but I was hoping for more.

We expect certain irreducible minimums when we do business. We expect health care to be competent. (According to one expert on health care, approximately one hundred thousand people die from medical errors each year, and half a million people are injured as a result of mistakes.) We expect financial advice to be accurate and helpful. We expect our employers to pay us.

But that isn't all we expect. Most of us have a litany of other expectations (see chapter 9 about the importance of experiences). And if we only get the bare basics, we expect to pay only the bare minimum. No matter how good a service rep may be, a poor technician can undo his or her best efforts. No matter how committed a bank teller may be, a manager can demoralize that individual or short-circuit his or her best efforts by implementing ineffective policies.

Being a Fred isn't about the job you hold but how you do the job.

Being a Fred isn't about the job you hold but how you do the job. Freds can be in any department, and in the best organizations they are in *every* department.

FRED DRIVES A FORKLIFT

Scholastic Inc. has been in business for more than ninety years. With $2 billion in revenue and more than nine thousand employees in sixteen countries, the company's mission is to help keep books alive. Scholastic is clear about its commitment to children's best educational interests.

Is that an issue at the leadership level only? Is it merely a marketing mantra? It could be, but in this case it informs and inspires employees throughout the organization.

Richard Robinson, president and CEO of the company, asked a forklift driver at a distribution center, "What is your job?" The employee didn't mention his forklift or distribution. He said, "My job is to help children love to read."

Great leaders and organizations know that if you have the right mission, forklifts and distribution centers are means to a greater end.

FRED THROWS BIRTHDAY PARTIES

Dr. Matt Messina is a dentist in Ohio. We met many years ago at a dental association meeting. I asked him how he applies the Fred principles in his practice. Here's what he shared with me: "As an office, we succeed because I have consummate professionals, and I let them do their best. My staff began looking for elderly patients in the schedule with appointments near their birthdays. They started stocking cupcakes and candles and made a point of singing 'Happy Birthday' for the patients at the end of their appointments."

A smile came across Dr. Messina's face. "There's nothing as heartwarming as seeing an eighty-seven-year-old man cry because someone remembered his birthday. We discovered that he had no family nearby and thought his birthday would pass without any fanfare. We have learned so much about our patients, their family birthday traditions, their joys, and their sorrows. People began to intentionally schedule appointments on their birthdays."

That is the nature of Fred.

FRED CUTS MEAT

After reading *The Fred Factor*, Jim Hunsicker shared this story with me in an e-mail.

I went to a local membership store to get meat for a holiday. I had called them earlier in the week, and they assured me they had tons of brisket—no problem.

The story changed when I was there at 7 a.m. one morning and they were fresh out. So I called my local grocer and asked to speak to the meat department. They quickly connected me to Kurvis, the meat department manager. He said he had plenty of meat, albeit at a higher price than the membership store, but that I should come see him.

I met Kurvis, and what a nice guy! He didn't have the amount of meat I needed packed yet, so he asked exactly what I wanted and told me to come back in ten minutes. He had it done in five minutes—and with a smile! When I told him how I wanted to prepare the meat, he helped me with spices and even directed me to the cooking bags.

I thanked him, and after I paid, I found the manager of the store and recognized him as a Fred. Sure enough, the store manager had read your book—not a shocker! Long story short: Freds are everywhere.

Jim paid a little more, but he got more than he had expected, and that made all the difference.

FRED IS A PET SANTA

Mae Wiggins works at a veterinary office and pet resort. She was reading *The Fred Factor* and wrote to tell me about her experience.

I work on the lodging side of the office. I love working with the animals and have been there for almost five years. After reading your book, I now know there's a name for the extra things I do for people and animals. It's called being a Fred.

I give Christmas cards and birthday cards to the dogs and cats that lodge with us. Yes—to the animals. The owners really enjoy it. I also make pet treats and give them out at Christmastime. I have always done extra things for people, and I enjoy helping out however I can. I try to wake up with a smile and see the good things in life.

Mae's love for the animals she cares for reflects the way she values their owners. The extras she provides enrich their experiences and keep them coming back.

FRED IS IN YOUR HOME

The spirit of Fred is about being of service to those we work and live with.

I recently received an e-mail from Eddie, a longtime colleague of mine. He explained that he wasn't as involved in our professional association as he used to be and then explained why. His mother, age ninety-two, is a victim of Alzheimer's disease. His father died of a medical error a while back, so Eddie now coordinates his mother's care.

He explained, "My brother and I often discuss how Mom was always there for us. Now it's time for us to be there for her."

I doubt my friend considers himself a Fred. He is simply doing what he thinks a good son who loves his aging mother should do. He's glad to provide the care for her that she provided for him throughout his life.

Fred may not be in the customer service department, but you'll always find him serving others.

At the end of the day, practicing the Fred Factor is about

being of great service, building better relationships, and creating new value—regardless of what department you work in or what your job description says.

....

ACTION STEPS

1. Think of an organization you've had contact with lately that disappointed you by providing ineffective or unhelpful service. If you had been part of the organization, what could you have done to meet and exceed expectations?

2. Think of an organization that has provided you with excellent service recently. Contact the company and let them know about the employee who demonstrated Fred-like service. Consider sharing with your coworkers what you experienced in order to encourage and inspire them.

3. Take one small step today—at home or at work—to go the extra mile in a service you provide.

CHAPTER 4

START WITH COMMITMENT

*The only happy people I know are the ones who are working
well at something they consider important.*

ABRAHAM MASLOW

IT'S NOT ALWAYS easy being a Fred. It takes commitment. But that commitment gets easier as time goes on. Why? Here's Fred's secret: the person who benefits most when you act like a Fred is *you.*

At the beginning, the Fred commitment might take some extra effort. Once you start reaping the rewards, though, you'll realize it's well worth it.

I have to admit that for years when I first started telling Fred's story, I was afraid the U.S. Postal Service would find out what he was doing and make him stop. For Fred, who is still delivering extraordinary service after thirty-five years at his job, it's not about a paycheck or pleasing his boss. He does what he does because it's the right thing to do. And he reaps the rewards of happiness, pride, and fulfillment.

Not everyone shares this sentiment—especially in the business world.

I often hear employees make statements like this: "I'll do

more when they pay me more." Of course, rarely is anyone paid more until they do more. The prevailing spirit of the age seems to be "Get before you give." Without a tangible incentive— money, recognition, or applause—many people just don't find any reason to do more than necessary.

And sometimes even when you do more, nobody notices. You don't get paid more, and you don't get a promotion! So why do an extraordinary job?

Where you work (whether or not you work for an employer who recognizes and rewards good performance) is a separate issue from *how* you work. You work in your current job either by choice or by need. In a perfect world there would be a clear link between pay and performance, but we don't live in a perfect world.

All Freds do ordinary work. Why? Because that's the only kind of work there is.

There isn't much you can do about your employer's payment practices or recognition policies. But here is a radical idea: Why not do the best job you can do for yourself and for others? You will find that being committed to the Fred way brings its own rewards—rewards that money can't buy.

WHAT ALL FREDS HAVE IN COMMON

All Freds do ordinary work. Why? Because that's the only kind of work there is. A physicist may do work that seems exotic to you, but to the physicist it is merely a series of ordinary tasks, done day after day, week after week.

All any of us have are ordinary days and ordinary work. But we have a choice about how we will do that work. If we commit to an attitude of service and excellence, our ordinary tasks will become extraordinary. It's only when we allow our work to become monotonous that it is truly ordinary.

All Freds have the same raw material: time, effort, and talent. Those are the building blocks for creating the extraordinary. The magic isn't in the materials but in how the materials are used.

WOULD YOU MOP A STRANGER'S FLOOR?

Edgar Ramirez has the commitment of a Fred. He shared this story with me after reading *The Fred Factor*:

> I stopped off at a gas station on Interstate 20 going east. All this time the principles of the book were operating in my heart and mind. After fueling the vehicle, I entered the station to use the restroom. Unfortunately the toilet malfunctioned and flooded. The attendant kindly said, "Sir, don't worry. I will take care of it."
>
> The Fred in me requested the mop. She handed it to me, and I saw a complete stranger (the Fred in me) joyfully mop up almost her entire store. As a result, the attendant invited my entire family and me to eat some delicious Middle Eastern cuisine. The attendant didn't realize that I had been influenced by your awesome book *The Fred Factor*.

Why did Edgar mop the floor? He didn't have to.
No, he simply wanted to. He enjoyed being of service.
Some people might think his actions were silly or over the top. A common reaction in a situation like this would be to say,

"Not me! Are you kidding? Why would I want to mop the floor of some business?"

But Edgar saw an opportunity for service where others might have seen drudgery. Don't confuse his generosity of spirit with being servile—he did it because he wanted to, not because he had to. And as you probably can tell from Edgar's letter, his Fred gesture not only made the attendant's day—it made Edgar's day too!

Ted Williams famously took each at bat as seriously as the one before. He said he knew there was always some kid in the crowd who was seeing him play for the first and only time. He wanted that kid to see what Ted Williams was all about, so he applied himself fully at each at bat.

In doing so, he gave more to his employers than many of his colleagues did. His reward? He's still considered the greatest hitter of all time and was admired by millions of fans throughout his life. But his even greater reward was the knowledge that he had done his best—every single time.

WHY BE A FRED?

There is an old saying that you should "count the cost before you make the commitment." But it is also helpful to understand the benefits that your commitment will create. Consider these eight benefits that come from a commitment to the Fred philosophy.

1. **Being a Fred enriches others.** It adds value to your relationships—your family, your coworkers, and the people you happen to meet as you make your way through the day.

2. **Being a Fred expands you.** When you go outside yourself, it changes the way you view and treat everyone you meet. In a virtuous cycle of enriching others, you'll find your own life enriched.

3. **Being a Fred puts more life into your living.** By proactively living each moment and by being fully engaged with others, you will discover a life that is happier, more meaningful, and more vivid.

4. **Being a Fred breaks the bonds of self-absorption.** Too often we get lost in our own needs, complaints, and problems. Doing Fred-like deeds for others gets you out of the rut of thinking about *me, me, me.*

5. **Being a Fred makes you more employable.** Employers want to hire people who are motivated and creative and show initiative. That's Fred!

6. **Being a Fred offers you a better way to live.** Everyone encounters obstacles, problems, and setbacks. You can wallow in what you can't do, or you can choose the Fred way and focus on the positive things you can do.

7. **Being a Fred creates positive influence.** Most of our lives are made up of interactions with others. If you constantly strive to improve those interactions, you not only improve the quality of life for other people, but also become a positive example. They may choose

to pass it on, and the Fred way will spread beyond your small corner of the world.

8. **Being a Fred is more fun.** When you're living the Fred way, people are glad to see you. They may even want to return a kindness you have paid them. Going through a day that way is just more fun than the ordinary alternative.

When you do something good—at home or at work—and you do it for the right reasons, you can't help but benefit.

COMMITMENT IS A DECISION, NOT A FEELING

There are days when you won't feel committed. You're not alone in that; it happens to everyone. The secret to lasting commitment is to make sure it's based on a rational decision, not just fleeting emotions.

At the most basic level, a commitment is a promise or a pledge you make to others or to yourself. On a legal level, a commitment can even take the form of a contract. On a personal level, commitment means a strong engagement or involvement with someone or something. But the common thread is the same: commitments require the daily decision to stick with them.

So commit to making a difference. Be more engaged in your relationships. Make a pledge to reinvent yourself. Make a contract with yourself to create value for others. Your payment? Happiness, healthy pride, and fulfillment.

THE THREE CHARACTERISTICS OF COMMITTED PEOPLE

1. COMMITTED PEOPLE ARE GENERALLY HAPPY.

I've rarely met an unhappy Fred. I've met some who felt under-appreciated, taken for granted, or frustrated, but it strikes me that overall, people who embrace these ideas and do business like Fred the Postman are a happy group of people.

You could argue that happy people are more likely to behave like Fred, not that they get happy because they behave like Fred. I prefer to think of it as a virtuous cycle: one reinforces the other.

Not everything we must do each day—at home or at work—makes us happy. In those cases we need to remember that how we choose to do anything has a significant influence on the emotions we experience. Doing an unpleasant task cheerfully trumps doing a pleasant task begrudgingly.

But let's not forget that there's plenty of space in our lives to choose to do the things that make us happy. Fred the Postman likes people. He likes being outdoors. He likes being of service. In a way, he is happy because he's doing what makes him happy—it's that virtuous cycle.

2. COMMITTED PEOPLE ARE CLEAR ABOUT WHAT THEY DO AND WHY THEY DO IT.

A. W. Tozer said, "It is not what a man does that determines whether his work is sacred or secular, it is why he does it." In other words, motives matter.

What you do to make a difference is important, but so is the reason you do it. You can do the right things for the wrong reasons (which is usually preferable to doing the wrong things for the right reasons).

As I've met and interviewed Freds around the world, I've noticed a common thread: few of them are motivated by recognition, money, or advancement. While they often appreciate those things, they aren't motivated by them.

When I ask, "Why do you do it?" I get answers like these:

"I enjoy it."

"Because I believe it's the right thing to do."

"It challenges me and keeps my work from becoming boring."

"I like helping others."

"This is the way I was raised."

"It's rewarding."

"I feel good when I'm of service."

Here are the reasons I rarely hear:

"I do it for the recognition."

"I do it to get ahead."

"My boss made me." (Actually, undue pressure from management can result in the opposite behavior from what's desired.)

"I had no choice."

It's true that providing great value as an individual or an organization often results in great benefits to the provider. But even if it doesn't, the reward is in the doing. Author Tim Ferriss calls this the power of process over outcome. If you set out to do something for a benefit or a payoff that doesn't happen, you feel like you've wasted your time, and you're disappointed if you don't get it.

However, if you set out to do something because you'll enjoy doing it regardless of the outcome, then any kind of tangible reward is icing on the cake. The process itself is the reward.

I can vouch for that thinking. If you set out to write a best-selling book, well, good luck. More than 280,000 new books are published each year, and only a tiny fraction attain bestseller status. In contrast, if you set out to write the best book you can and your aim is to enjoy the writing process and help the reader, then your happiness and success don't hinge on making any list.

Motives can short-circuit efforts and outcomes. Early in the green movement, some companies saw being eco-friendly first as a terrific marketing opportunity and then as the right thing to do. They thought that if they could convince people that their organizations were green, they would increase sales and market share. Today, the companies that are committed to sustainability as a genuine value seem to be doing much better in the loyalty and revenue department than those that are merely going through the motions.

> **A commitment without a goal is like a trip without a map: odds are you won't get to where you want to be.**

3. COMMITTED PEOPLE HAVE GOALS.

A commitment without a goal is like a trip without a map: odds are you won't get to where you want to be.

A distinction of commitment is the desire to make a mark

in life—not just any mark, but an extraordinary, positive mark. Knowing the kind of difference you hope to make greatly increases the likelihood of success.

What kind of difference do you want to make? Whom do you hope to influence? When will you start? These are all questions a Fred needs to answer.

Set a goal to add value, enrich a relationship, or make a difference in your work, your home, or your community in the next two weeks.

Write it down—no excuses. I have learned that if you aren't willing to take the time to write something down, odds are you won't be willing to make the time to do it.

Here's a two-way test: if you are truly committed, you'll bring enthusiasm and positive expectancy to what you do beyond what is expected. The second part of the test is that when it comes time to act, you will follow through, regardless of your feelings. If you don't, you may not be as committed as you thought you were.

I know this from personal experience. I can commit to writing a blog post, giving a speech, or taking my sons fishing (all things I usually enjoy), but if the day arrives and I'm "not in the mood," I'm not entitled to a free pass. If I fail to follow through, my readers, my audience, and my kids know I'm a poser.

The goals you achieve prove and bolster the commitment you've made. Be definitive in what you're going to commit to in order to turn the ordinary into the extraordinary.

★

When you take the step from being merely involved to being truly committed, everyone benefits—your company, your family, and especially you. As Vince Lombardi said, "The quality of a person's life is in direct proportion to their commitment to excellence, regardless of their chosen field of endeavor."

GOAL SETTING

Post the goal you've written beside your phone or your alarm clock so you'll see it when you wake up in the morning. At the beginning of each day, think through the smaller steps you need to take to accomplish that goal. At the end of the day, reflect on the progress you made. Taking time to be intentional at the beginning and end of each day is a simple but powerful tool in achieving your goals.

CHAPTER 5

WORK WITH PASSION

Remarkable contributions are spawned by a passionate commitment
to transcendent human values, such as beauty, truth, wisdom, justice,
charity, fidelity, joy, courage, and honor.

GARY HAMEL

TRAVIS PASTRANA was well known as an X Games champion
and a hero to many. Recently, however, he made a move to
NASCAR. The company was ecstatic, because they wanted
to attract a younger fan base—the next generation—and they
thought fans would follow Pastrana. To their surprise, though,
the fans didn't come.

Pastrana was surprised too. After communicating with his
fans, he determined that many of them thought he'd sold out—
that he'd gone to NASCAR for the money.

He quickly let them know that it wasn't about the money;
for him, it was about the challenge. He wanted to learn new
skills and broaden his involvement in motor sports. Once he
communicated that sincerely, his fans reengaged.

The lesson? For businesses, profit is important. But for the
people who work in those businesses and the people who buy
from them, profit isn't enough. Passion should come before profit.

Being a Fred is possible only if you have the right purpose and are driven by your passion. Doing less is seen as inauthentic. Don't fake it until you make it. Make it by getting excited about doing the things you value. That's what creates value for others, too.

But before we can commit to working with passion, we need to understand what that actually means. Passion isn't about doing only the things we like to do, because that isn't real life. We all do things that we have to do—the necessities.

Passion should come before profit.

The problem is when we *only* do the necessities and don't do anything we're passionate about.

Passion is about arranging your work and your life as much as possible to do the things you are passionate about as often as you can.

For example, I'm passionate about learning, so I schedule that into my life, whether it's by reading books and periodicals or by attending conferences that stretch my thinking. I'm passionate about speaking, but not so much about getting on airplanes and staying in hotel rooms away from my family. However, I've decided that's a price I'm willing to pay to pursue my passion.

What are you passionate about?

PRACTICAL PASSION

The overarching definition of *passion* is an intense, compelling emotion; a strong feeling; a desire for something.

It's interesting to note that the story of Christ's crucifixion is often referred to as the Passion. That's because the word originated from the Greek word for suffering and submission.

Suffering and submission? Really?

Yes, because true passion demands something from us. It requires a sacrifice on our part. If we're really passionate about something, we're happy to invest our time and money and energy in it. In fact, that's one of the tests to help us determine what our passion is—whether we're willing to pour ourselves into it. In short, passion is something we're willing to give ourselves to despite the cost.

HOW CAN YOU FIND YOUR PASSION?

Here are some questions to prompt your thinking about what you're passionate about.

1. WHAT WOULD YOU DO FOR FREE?
Is there an activity you enjoy so much that you'd do it for free, even if other people would consider it work?

A friend of mine enjoys writing so much that he offers to write grants for nonprofit organizations at no charge. Most people consider grant writing drudgery, but my friend is happiest when he's writing. He manages to follow his passion while benefiting worthy causes at the same time.

2. WHAT RILES YOU?
Irritation can be a great motivator. Are there problems or annoyances that drive you up the wall? Perhaps you can find your passion in fixing them.

A woman who lived in a nice neighborhood was upset that

there was no place for kids to play. She was annoyed that city planners had thought of everything except the children. So she turned her aggravation into action, organized her neighbors, and after several years of dedicated work, got a playground built in her neighborhood. By converting her annoyance into a passion, she created great value for her community.

3. WHAT INTERESTS YOU?

What do you like to read about and study? When you're in a bookstore or at a newsstand or browsing online, what piques your interest? Do you find yourself returning to the same topics again and again? Perhaps you've found your passion. Your heart may be telling you what it wants; you just need to recognize it.

4. WHO INTERESTS YOU?

What groups of people do you tend to notice? That is, whom are you most interested in helping? Are you drawn to coach, counsel, encourage, or teach? Some people have a heart for young children. Others volunteer their time to help those who are underprivileged or live on the streets. Other people like to support young entrepreneurs. I know several retired business leaders who enjoy mentoring managers. Find out what demographic you're wired to connect with.

5. WHAT WILL MINIMIZE YOUR REGRETS?

If you have regrets at the end of your life, what do you think they'll be? We tend to ask ourselves, *Will I regret doing this?* But often the better question is, *Will I regret* not *doing this?*

The most common workplace regrets I hear are from people who get to the end of their careers and feel like they dedicated their lives to work they didn't think was important or they wasted their time just to make money.

There are two main kinds of regrets: things we wish we hadn't done (bad decisions) and things we wish we had done (unfulfilled desires). But regret minimization means more than being aware of what we want to accomplish and more than being able to anticipate what we will wish we had or hadn't done. Minimizing regret means being able to seize the moment when opportunity arises. We can do this only when we're clear about what is both important and worthy to us.

Take a moment to inventory your life to date. What might you regret if nothing changes? Project into the future when a child, grandchild, or other family member asks, "What would you have done differently?" Knowing how you might answer in the future will provide insight into what you can do now.

PASSION ISN'T THE ONLY THING

As powerful as passion is, it won't accomplish much on its own. Remember, the roots of passion are submission and sacrifice. If you don't put your all—your commitment, your hard work, and your focus—into your passion, you won't be able to achieve your goals.

Larry Winget, also known as the Pitbull of Personal Development, is a longtime friend and colleague. Here's what he had to say about passion in a recent commencement speech he gave:

> It's about work and excellence. Regardless of what others may tell you, it's not about your passion—

as I know people who are passionately incompetent. It's not loving what you do or being happy every day. You aren't paid to be happy on the job; you are paid to do your job. Success always comes down to hard work and excellence. And it takes both. Hard work alone won't cut it. I know people who work really hard yet aren't any good at what they do, so it doesn't matter. And I know people who are excellent at what they do but they don't work hard enough at it to make any difference.

This might surprise you, but I agree.

Notice that Larry didn't say he's opposed to passion. He's opposed to *only* passion. Passion isn't a substitute for competence. Passion can't replace hard work. Passion can't be swapped for commitment. Passion isn't more important than value.

Once you have the philosophy (you know what matters not only to you but also to your employer and your customers) and you develop the skills (you are competent to accomplish the task), then you've got a burning fire. In some fields, such as medicine, would-be professionals must complete more than a decade of schooling and residencies before they can practice on their own. When it comes to having major surgery or getting your car's engine fixed, it isn't enough to have someone who is passionate about his or her job. That person also needs to be skilled and committed.

Passion without commitment and hard work is like a cart without a horse—it's not going anywhere.

While few people are passionate about every aspect of their

education, they know it is part of the cost. Their passion drives them to submit and suffer through the necessary training to reach their goals.

Passion without commitment and hard work is like a cart without a horse—it's not going anywhere. When you watch someone like Fred Shea or "Brother Love" Mike Flowers on their delivery routes, you can tell they're passionate about their jobs based on the enthusiasm they bring, the value they add, and the relationships they build.

THE DIFFERENCE BETWEEN ORDINARY AND EXTRAORDINARY

Passion makes the difference between something common and something special. When you walk into an ordinary restaurant, you probably expect a good meal and adequate service. But contrast that experience with dining at a family-run bistro where someone cooks with real passion and care, where they have created a special environment. That's the value passion can add.

In a perfect world, we'd all get paid for what we do based on how passionate we are about it. The real world, of course, doesn't work like that. But you *can* find your passions and pursue them, regardless of your circumstances. Work hard at them. Get better at them. Look for opportunities, large or small, to bring what you value to your life and work. Then look for opportunities to make your passions your life and work.

Apple cofounder Steve Jobs summed up the importance of passion, even in the face of adversity: "Sometimes life hits you in the head with a brick. Don't lose faith. I'm convinced that the only thing that kept me going was that I loved what I did. You've got to find what you love."

....

UNCOVERING YOUR PASSIONS

1. What do you love to do so much that you'd do it for free?

2. What irritates you enough to make you want to take action?

3. What fields of study interest you most?

4. Are there certain groups of people you tend to be drawn to? Children? The elderly? The underprivileged?

5. What do you want to be remembered for?

6. What would you do if you had unlimited resources?

Take one small step today to make one of these passions closer to reality in your life.

CHAPTER 6

CULTIVATE YOUR CREATIVITY

Thought is the sculptor who can create the person you want to be.
HENRY DAVID THOREAU

ONE OF THE THINGS that sets Fred Shea apart is that he does his job with creativity.

I'm not sure he thinks of himself as creative, but Fred took the ordinary—dare I say potentially dull?—job of delivering the mail and made it artistry. He didn't overhaul how the mail was delivered to his customers' boxes; he simply *improved* his part in the process. He was thoughtful about adding a few extra touches to increase the value of his service.

Critics of the book think Fred must work extra hours each day.

"Are you kidding?" Fred said. "What I do takes very little extra time at all. For instance, how long does it take to pick up a newspaper lying on the sidewalk and put it on the porch?"

Creativity is an essential ingredient in delivering extraordinary results like Fred does.

I've heard from a number of people over the years who feel

they can't keep delivering extraordinary results because they don't consider themselves to be creative.

"I'm committed and passionate about what I do," they've told me. "But creative? That's just not me!"

Perhaps many of us tend to respond this way because when we think of creativity, we immediately picture artists like Picasso or Van Gogh. True, they were uber-creative. But creativity is not reserved only for those who make museum-quality masterpieces. More often, creativity takes the form of a new solution, a flourish, a personalized touch, or a different way of doing things.

The simplest definition of creativity is producing something new or different that has value. That's the key: doing things that others value. By definition, then, to be creative is to offer value to those you live with and work with. To be creative in your work and personal life is to be, well, a Fred.

Creativity isn't just about macro-level ideas that come from the top of an organization. It also encompasses our smaller daily routines. For example, creativity could be as simple as finding a novel way to greet the people you meet each day to let them know you're not just going through the motions.

The important question is not, how creative am I? but how can I be creative?

About fifteen years ago, a group of Harvard psychiatrists studied the importance of "everyday creativity." They found that people who exercise creativity in their daily lives are happier, healthier, and more productive.

So don't worry if you aren't an artist or a poet. You may not even feel like you have creative tendencies. No matter. The important question is not, how creative am I? but how can I be creative? In other words, how can you create new value for yourself and those around you?

Here are a few simple ways to jump-start your everyday creativity:

1. THINK AGAIN.

Don't underestimate the value of second, third, and fourth thoughts.

When students take standardized tests, teachers tell them that their first answer is usually the best one. But real life isn't a multiple-choice test. In our jobs and home life, our first answer is often to do things the way they've always been done. But the best solution may lie elsewhere. And we may not arrive at it until we've thought about the problem two or three or even four different ways.

If this approach doesn't come naturally for you, try thinking about a problem from the perspective of your customer, your coworker, or your spouse. Instead of considering what would be easiest and most familiar to you, think about what would be the best solution for them. Another way to bolster creativity is to consider doing your duties or chores in a different order. Would a different routine make you more efficient? Simply *thinking again* about the daily matters we take for granted will spur some creative thoughts—and just may lead to added value.

A friend of mine started a new job as a school administrator. One of his first major tasks was to send out information to new students. Like the administrators before him, he gathered the usual documents from different departments, packaged them up, and sent them out. Soon after, many new students called with questions that should have been answered in the information in the packet.

He decided to take a second look at the packet. He realized that new students opened the envelope to find a pile of loose papers, with no guide as to which ones were important or what to look at first. His intent was to send them a guide to enrollment, but instead he sent them a puzzle to piece together.

After thinking a second and a third time about the way students saw the mailer, he decided that "the way things had always been done" was not working. He set out to reorganize the packet and bind it together as a user's manual. The first page explained to students how to use their new "product"—their new school. The confused calls and complaints disappeared, and my friend was promoted within a year.

My friend used his creativity to rethink a well established procedure by imagining how others would experience his work. In the process, he created something of value to students, parents, and colleagues.

Are there routines and tasks in your life and work that could be improved by exercising your everyday creativity? Do you tend to solve problems by implementing the same solutions that have always been used? Try thinking again. And again. And again. Those second, third, and fourth thoughts just might create some value.

2. NOODLE ON IT.

Noodling is my favorite slang word for letting little ideas simmer.

In a world of instant gratification, the art of contemplation is out of fashion. Too often we try to apply this "quick fix" approach to issues we face in life and work. When we encounter a problem, we feel like *JEOPARDY!* contestants—as if we have to buzz in within seconds with the correct answer. Creativity, however, rarely emerges under such pressure.

Other times we may give ourselves time to think about a situation, but we focus so intently on the problem that we don't allow our creative minds the time and space to come up with a solution.

This might sound counterintuitive when you're trying to be productive, but rest and downtime go hand in hand with creativity. If you want your brain to do your work for you, you have to treat it right. You may only come up with the solution after you've given your mind a chance to relax and stretch out. In fact, psychologists tell us that our deepest sleep, REM, enhances our creative problem-solving abilities. So you just may need to sleep on it!

Creativity rarely emerges under pressure.

If you aren't able to sleep on it, give yourself a break and daydream a little. Intentionally let go of the problem for a little while, and think about it at different times of the day. You never know when and where creativity will strike, and you'll find yourself saying, "Of course! That's the solution!" The answer often comes at a time when you aren't actively thinking about it—almost as if your creative mind is working for you while the rest of your brain has some time off. If you're anything like me, your creative solutions might come to you in the shower!

3. IF YOU DON'T KNOW, ASK.

Creativity often comes from asking questions—of ourselves and of others.

Ask simple questions, like, is there a better way to do this?

or why has it always been done this way? More often than not, these simple questions will spark some creativity, and that creativity will create value. But you won't know until you ask!

One of your team members may have a creative solution but won't offer it until someone asks for his or her opinion. By asking the question, you bring that team member's creativity out into the open, where everyone can benefit from the value.

Likewise, your customers are the best evaluators of your business. More than anyone else, they know what they want from you, what you do well, and what you could do better. However, most of them won't provide that information unless they're asked. If you don't ask the question, you don't get the answer—or the value that answer might create.

If you're not sure where to begin, here are a few questions to get you started:

Ask yourself, "What have I always wanted to do differently in my job?"

Ask your team, "Why do we do things the way we do? What are some suggestions for how we can improve?"

Ask your manager, "How can I add value to my work?"

Ask your customers, "What can we do to be of greater service? What can we do as a company to improve?"

I've always wondered why in some hotels, the housekeeping staff put the stopper down in the bathtub. That requires guests to lift the stopper to keep the tub from filling when they're taking a shower. Personally, I'd rather reach into a vat of nuclear waste than touch the stopper in a hotel tub. That is the opposite of a value add; it is a value detract.

So recently when I encountered this situation at a nice hotel, I asked the staff, "Why?"

Their response? "We don't know, but we should find out."

What are the tub stopper concerns your customers have? Why not ask them?

4. GO BACK TO THE DRAWING BOARD.

Sometimes we get stuck when we keep doing what we've always done.

When we encounter a problem, the easiest approach seems to be the one that has been tried before. The safety of the "tried and true" often keeps us from attempting something new. Even if the "road less traveled" might be the best solution, we're reluctant to try it because it would mean starting from scratch.

But what would happen if we started with a clean slate? Sometimes a fresh start is exactly what we need to reach our goal. When navigating a maze, we may make a lot of progress, turn by turn, only to reach a dead end. Usually the way out of a dead end is not just to go back a couple of turns. Instead, we need to start over from the beginning so we can steer away from the roadblocks we hit the first time around until we ultimately reach our destination.

5. USE "CREATIVE SPARKS."

The inspiration for creativity can come from anywhere. When you come across something that stimulates your thinking, chances are it will do the same for others. So look for inspiration and then take time to share it—whether it comes in the form of pithy quotes, insightful articles, funny videos, or inspiring images.

When you bring a conversation piece or something thought provoking to work, it helps disrupt the daily grind—yours and everyone else's.

6. BREAK THE RULES.

Conventional wisdom controls much of what we do. These little rules usually start with someone saying, "Everyone knows . . ." or "They always say . . ." For example, conventional wisdom says, "Neither a borrower nor a lender be" or "Don't go out on a limb." But are "they" always right? One of the most meaningful gestures a stranger ever made to me was when a hotel employee loaned me enough money to get to the airport for my flight home. I'll never forget him. He was a Fred.

One client of mine was operating under the conventional wisdom that all customers wanted "one-stop service." But the customers still weren't getting the results they wanted. So the company did some research and found out that what people really wanted was "one-person" service—one go-to person they knew they could count on for everything. If they hadn't questioned the "rules," they might never have found the solution.

7. ADD AND SUBTRACT.

Give more of what your customers want, and get rid of what they don't want.

Adding a little something could be just what you or your company needs to do to deliver excellent service. One of my favorite barbecue restaurants makes free soft-serve ice cream cones available to every guest. It doesn't cost them much, but patrons love it. Sometimes one more person, one more gesture, or one extra bit of effort is all that's necessary to get the job done well.

Sometimes a solution you're working on might be one step too complicated. Are there unnecessary hoops that you or your customers are jumping through that could be eliminated? Have you gone overboard in a way that turns some off?

A successful online boutique eyeglass shop found that some customers thought the logos on the front of their lenses made them feel like walking billboards. The company took off the logos and put the branding on the frames instead.

Take a few minutes to think creatively about how addition or subtraction might be all you need to solve a problem or improve your daily life and work.

8. VIEW THE PROBLEM THROUGH A DIFFERENT LENS.

You can learn while on vacation. How is the problem you're facing solved in Mexico or in Europe? Even if you physically can't travel, think about how you might solve your problem if you lived in the Caribbean or in Scandinavia. Psychologically distant thoughts will spur your creativity.

You don't have to leave town to use a different lens. Visit a retailer, a museum, an auto dealer, a library, or a business different from your own. Look for ideas they're using successfully, and find a way to adapt them to your work.

9. CONVERT YOUR IDEAS INTO ACTIONS.

One of the biggest barriers to creativity is moving a solution from an idea to an action. You need to take it from concept to practice. The best way to make that translation is to ask yourself, *What Would That Look Like (WWTLL)?* That question forces you to define the inputs and outputs—the things you need to do to get the results you desire.

And if your idea comes out of left field and seems far fetched, asking WWTLL will enable you to determine if it is doable.

10. SHAKE IT UP!

Our mundane routines can be enemies of creativity. So intentionally change things up. Take a different route to work one day. Try a new flavor of coffee or tea. Have lunch with a friend or colleague you don't talk to often. Periodically doing things differently will keep you from getting bored and will spur your creativity.

You can also use this technique to get around the little problems that plague your day. For example, if someone says something that usually annoys you, try reacting in a different way by saying something positive in response. This might result in a chain reaction that makes your job a lot more pleasant.

There's always more than one way to think about a problem. Now you have ten! Using these creative techniques will help you create value for those around you. You may surprise yourself, and you may surprise them, too. And that's exactly what it means to be a Fred.

....

CREATIVITY IN ACTION

Think of a specific problem that has you stumped or an opportunity you'd like to maximize, whether at work or at home. Apply some of the strategies outlined in this chapter to jump-start your creativity.

Problem:

1. Rethink the problem, going beyond your initial reaction.

2. Take a break, go for a walk, or spend some time daydreaming before coming back to the dilemma again.

3. Ask a few key people for their opinions about the situation.

4. Scratch what you've done in the past and rethink the process from the beginning.

5. Ask your customers what they like and don't like about the way you've conventionally treated this situation.

6. Get rid of or add one thing to your current process for handling this issue.

7. Visit an individual or an organization that is handling this situation well and get tips from them.

Action Steps:

CHAPTER 7

DEVELOP YOUR DIFFERENCE

It's easy to make a buck. It's a lot tougher to make a difference.
TOM BROKAW

MANY YEARS AGO I met a sincere manager who shared with me that he had a habit of ending each day at work by asking the members of his team, "Did you make a difference today?" He wanted to remind them of the impact they could have on others.

I appreciated his intent, but I have come to believe that his question wasn't the best one to ask. A better question would be, "What kind of difference did you make today?"

Whether we realize it or not, we leave an impact every day—for better or for worse. Everything we do affects those around us in little or big ways, either enriching their lives or diminishing them.

It's our choice whether we'll use our time, effort, and talents to turn ordinary work into something extraordinary. And as simple as it sounds, that's all it takes: a choice.

When it comes to our jobs, we actually have two choices to make:

Will we do meaningful work?

Will we make our work meaningful in the way we do it?

You're blessed if you feel like the work you do is truly meaningful and makes an important difference in the world. Most people don't have jobs with a grandiose purpose beyond the tasks they're assigned to do. That's when we're challenged to instill meaning into our work ourselves. The meaning may not be inherent in the work, but we still can do the right things for the right reasons—and for reasons that support our greater purpose and calling.

NOBODY IS NEUTRAL

Have you ever heard someone say that he or she is neutral? I remember doing a performance review in which the employee told me, "Look, I may not be doing a great job, but I'm not doing a bad job. I do what I'm told—I follow the rules and don't cause problems. I'm just neutral."

Indifference is the opposite of making a difference.

Consider the last time you interacted with someone. If that person was disinterested, didn't engage you, and didn't invest any energy in the conversation, did you evaluate him or her as neutral? Probably not. You likely saw that person as indifferent, and indifference is a primary killer of business, loyalty, and relationships.

Indifference is the enemy of initiative. According to Fred principles, *indifference* is the opposite of *making a difference*.

We all make a difference, from small to significant, in

our interactions each day. Being a Fred is about choosing to make a positive difference. Thinking proactively about how to make a bigger, better difference is at the heart of the Fred philosophy.

So what can you do to intentionally make a significant difference? You'll be most influential when your difference making is based on your unique abilities, desires, and passions. In other words, you can make *a* difference in the world, or you can commit to making *your* difference.

WHAT ABOUT "THEM"?

Them: the naysayers, critics, and curmudgeons who not only choose not to make a positive difference but also discourage you from and judge you for doing so.

I asked Fred the Postman for advice about negative coworkers. He said, "Keep on keeping on. Let criticism roll off your shoulders. They need your example."

He's absolutely right!

Many years ago I spoke to the staff of one of the top restaurants on the Las Vegas strip. Their reputation for both food and service was world renowned.

I assumed I'd be preaching to the converted when I talked about the Fred principles, but afterward a waitstaff employee pulled me aside.

"What you talked about is my philosophy too," she said. "I believe in the same principles and do my best to practice them each day. I'd never heard of *The Fred Factor* before, but I'm all about this approach to creating value for customers and others."

She took a breath and continued. "But I take a lot of heat for it. Some of the others here say I'm working too hard and making them look bad. They tell me to relax and be more like them. What should I do?"

I hate "happy talk," which I define as telling someone something that sounds good but is unrealistic or untrue. I wanted to shoot straight, so I said, "I hate to hear that. And I have to admit I'm a little surprised, knowing what I do about the restaurant. I've eaten here several times, and the service has always been impeccable, like the service you are committed to providing."

Then I addressed the key issue: "People are critical of others for any number of reasons, but it seems like you have a clue about the reason for the jealousy and criticism you get. Some of your coworkers think your service is making them look bad. They don't have the same enthusiasm and passion you do. Your good work is making their mediocre work apparent. So here's your choice: you can bow to their criticism and become mediocre too. Or you can use your best sense of humor to laugh it off and keep doing what's important to you."

That's the choice all of us have: bow to the critics or live by our own values. As an author, I get reviewed, and over the years I've received both positive and negative critiques. Of the bad reviews, some criticism is valid and some is simply mean spirited. I try to take away what I can from this feedback, but when it comes down to it, I can't make everybody happy. I just choose to do my work to provide as much value as I can, regardless of how it's received.

Like Fred says, keep on keeping on, and laugh your way past those who refuse to smile.

THE DIFFERENCE BETWEEN *A* DIFFERENCE AND *YOUR* DIFFERENCE

Everyone makes a difference; you can make a unique difference.

In order to be a Fred, it's not enough just to make a positive difference in the lives of others, although that's obviously a good and noble thing to do. Being a Fred means making a signature difference—in other words, combining the opportunity to be of significant service with your unique style and abilities.

We all have specific areas of strength and talent. Similarly, we all find ourselves in situations with unique needs. Applying our particular talents, while at the same time addressing the specific needs in our environment, is the way to make a signature difference.

Fred Shea makes a difference as a postman. While delivering the mail might seem mundane and ordinary, Fred takes advantage of his strengths and his circumstances to make a signature difference. For example, while mail in general might not be very relevant or interesting to most people, their own mail certainly is! Fred treats each person's mail with the significance he would assign if it were going to his own mailbox. I'm sure no one on Fred's route ever worries about their important gift, check, job notice, or health news going astray. That is one of Fred's signature differences.

Fred's seemingly ordinary job causes him to cross paths with dozens of people each day. That circumstance gives him the chance to do little things that make a difference in the lives of the residents on his route. And Fred doesn't miss the chance. His customers regularly get a cheery greeting, news about their mail, or some small kindness, like the placement of a newspaper or delivery at their doorstep. That's another way Fred uses his strengths and circumstances to make a signature difference.

Life is interesting when you aim to make a positive difference; I believe it's even more interesting when you strive to make a signature difference. You can make a unique contribution to the world around you, affecting everyone in your life and work for the better. But first you need to identify your signature difference.

DISCOVERING YOUR SIGNATURE DIFFERENCE

These four simple questions will help you uncover your signature difference and live it out.

1. WHAT IS YOUR UNIQUE STYLE?

Authenticity means being true to yourself. What is your temperament like? Are you bold and outgoing? Or are you quiet and even tempered in your approach?

When people describe you, what are the words they most often use?

Don't just think of your signature difference as the difference you want to make but also as an extension of what makes you different.

My friend Naomi Rhode is an encourager. She and her husband, Jim, have built a multifaceted business in the dental profession. But Naomi contributes something special to their business—her unique ability to care for people, encourage them, and lift them up. Clients, dental staff, friends, family, and colleagues all benefit from Naomi's signature difference.

2. WHAT ARE YOUR SIGNATURE STRENGTHS?

What do you see as your "best self"? What do others say your strengths are?

Knowing your strengths and talents will give you some clues as to the ways you can make the most significant difference. One lawyer I know who specializes in business negotiations offers his services as a mediator to individuals who can't afford legal representation. He has a gift for helping people resolve their differences, and he uses this skill as a way to give back to his community.

3. WHAT ARE YOUR TRUE PASSIONS?

In chapter 5 we talked about how to identify your passions. We might assume that the things we love are limited to our hobbies or our free time, but our passions can be the fuel to make a true difference in our world.

One friend of mine loves soccer. He watches the sport whenever he can and reads about it constantly. Recently he took a course in coaching soccer, and now he volunteers as a youth soccer coach. He converted his interest in the sport into the opportunity to make a difference for kids at the local YMCA.

4. WHAT DO YOU WANT TO BE REMEMBERED FOR?

Your legacy is what you will be remembered for. Think about what you might want to be known for after you're gone. Then ask yourself, *What did I do to build my legacy today? Did I make sure that everyone I crossed paths with will remember me the way I want to be remembered?*

You might want to be remembered as a kindhearted, decent person. Will the people you interact with today remember you that way? You also might want to be remembered for specific qualities and talents. Ted Williams said that when he passed by, he wanted people to say, "There goes the greatest hitter there ever was." So he worked tirelessly to make himself better and ensure that he gave each performance his all. As a result, he is remembered exactly the way he wanted to be remembered.

GIVE PEOPLE SOMETHING TO TALK ABOUT

Bonnie Raitt sang about giving them something to talk about. In the context of that song, she was referring to the feelings between two lovers. But no matter the context, people love to talk. They like to talk about what's right and what's wrong, who they like and who they don't like, and everything in between.

People are going to talk. That's just the nature of folks.

So what are you giving people to talk about when it comes to your signature difference? I'm not suggesting you devote your life to managing spin (the perceptions people have), but I do believe we are responsible for living in a way that shows others who we truly are and what we believe.

We are responsible for living in a way that shows others who we truly are and what we believe.

Those little changes you make each day are cumulative. The sum of your actions and interactions makes you admired or despised or something in between. People might see you as a Fred or as the opposite of a Fred.

The night before I spoke at an automobile dealership in Houston, Texas, I went to its Yelp site to find out the buzz about my client. There were glowing reviews from customers who had done business recently with the company. In addition to making general statements about the price of the cars, the newness of the facilities, and the wide selection of inventory, the reviews also focused on an employee within the dealership who did something extraordinary for the customer.

The next day after I spoke, a salesperson named Kenny approached me. "You talked about adding value and making a unique difference. I try to do that."

He opened a small bag of handmade key fobs woven together with brightly colored materials. "After I sell a car, I always give the buyers one of these, and they love it."

Kenny gets it. Nobody buys a $30,000 car to get a key fob. But I've purchased many cars over the years and never received a custom-made key fob like that before. Every time the owners start their cars, they think of Kenny. And who do you think they'll go to when they want to buy another vehicle?

BE INTENTIONALLY EXTRAORDINARY

The extraordinary doesn't just happen.

Picasso didn't accidentally paint impressionistic master-pieces. U2 doesn't accidentally write and perform music that moves millions of fans. The president of a country doesn't accidentally get elected to that position. Works of artistry, significance, and greatness are the product of intention. Being intentional about how you live and the kind of difference you want to make is the first step toward becoming extraordinary.

Live with intent. Let the difference you make be your signature difference.

DEFINING YOUR SIGNATURE DIFFERENCE

In order to make a signature difference, you need to find the intersection between your contributions and the needs of those around you. First, consider your unique style, strengths, and passions. Next, think about the needs of those around you—in your workplace, your family, your circle of friends, and your community.

Then write out your signature difference in the form of a personal commitment statement.

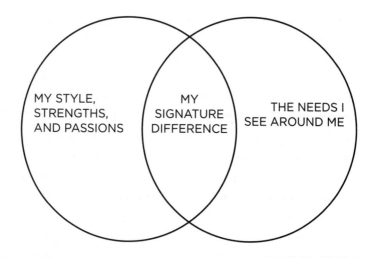

MY STYLE, STRENGTHS, AND PASSIONS

MY SIGNATURE DIFFERENCE

THE NEEDS I SEE AROUND ME

CHAPTER 8

BUILD BETTER RELATIONSHIPS

The NBA is never just a business. It's always business.
It's always personal. All good businesses are personal.
The best businesses are very personal.

MARK CUBAN

WHAT MAKES Fred Shea, my postal carrier, so exceptional? What makes anyone—regardless of their position or work—memorable and extraordinary? We are most impressed not just by the quality of a person's work but also by the way he or she treats us. Relationships are key.

In my view, Fred Shea stood out from other postal carriers who had served our neighborhood for many reasons, but the primary one was his sincere interest in getting to know me. How can you serve customers well if you don't know or understand them? Fred's influence came from his ability to relate to others and build genuine relationships with those on his route—including me.

What makes people like Fred the Postman so good with people is this simple thing: he treats people like friends. He doesn't wait to become friends with someone. He assumes the positive, expects the best, and values the other person. And guess what? The people he interacts with feel valued.

THE CONCERNED BARISTA

When someone you don't know expresses sincere concern for your well-being, it makes a lasting impression.

I love coffee, and Starbucks is practically an addiction for me. In June 2005, I was in downtown Fort Collins, Colorado (aka Fredville, USA), and ordered my favorite coffee from the barista. As I waited for her to make it, I asked her where I could find a *USA Today* newspaper.

"We don't sell them, but I think they sell them over there." She pointed across the busy intersection to several newspaper boxes.

As I grabbed my beverage and headed out the door, she yelled out, "Hey!"

I turned around, thinking I'd forgotten something.

She smiled. "Just be careful crossing the street."

What made my experience different that morning wasn't the physical store space or even the product. It was a sincere barista who wanted to make sure I didn't get run over by a bus while crossing the street.

TREAT 'EM LIKE TIM

I have spoken at two different leadership events with Tim Tebow, the NFL superstar of the Denver Broncos and the New York Jets.

The first time I shared the stage with him, our country was at the height of Tebow mania. People were drawn to Tim not just because of his athletic abilities (he was a new pro quarterback, just out of college) but also because of his integrity, his faith, and his commitment. Outside the event center, I saw at least two hundred people lining the sidewalk Tim would use to enter the venue. When he finally appeared, they cheered and high-fived him.

I remember thinking, *What if we treated everyone the way we treat Tim?* People might find it a bit odd if we cheered for our customers, colleagues, families, and friends, but what if we brought the same kind of energy to our important relationships that the crowd brought to the sidewalk that day?

After all, isn't that why we love our dogs? They're always thrilled to see us when we come home, and they greet us by wagging their tails and running in circles. We don't need to run in circles for our customers, but wouldn't it be nice if people could tell how much we valued them and their business?

TREAT PEOPLE BIG

At the other end of the spectrum from people like Fred are the downers—the people who never miss an opportunity to say something snide or to belittle someone else. In a one-on-one setting, diminishing people is a relationship killer. In a service setting, it's a business killer.

I encountered a downer one Sunday on my way home from church when I stopped at the store to pick up a few items. Since my son Jack was sick and had been eating a lot of soup, I picked up four cans of chicken noodle on impulse.

I didn't count how many items I had in my basket, but as I approached the "fifteen items or less" lane, I figured I was pretty close. To give you an idea of the scene, there was nobody behind me. It wasn't a busy day. And right next to me was another express lane.

As I was checking out, the cashier said quite loudly, "The number-of-items police aren't on duty today." He didn't appear to be talking to me—it was more of an aside meant for me to hear.

At this point, I was starting to think maybe the cashier was trying to lay a guilt trip on me. My suspicion was confirmed when he handed me the register tape and said, "Here's your *really long* receipt."

As I left the store, I worried that I had egregiously violated checkout etiquette. I must have had a hundred items to warrant such berating!

I did a quick count and realized I had twenty-two items (those pesky soup cans didn't help).

This incident occurred at the grocery store where I regularly shop, but it made me rethink whether I wanted to continue shopping there. Never underestimate what a relational interaction—positive or negative—can do for your business.

SIX STEPS TO BUILDING BETTER RELATIONSHIPS

You may be convinced that relationships are essential to the health of your business or organization, but you aren't sure how to strengthen the ones you have and build new ones. These steps will give you a place to start.

1. IT ISN'T ENOUGH TO BUILD RELATIONSHIPS IF YOU DON'T MAINTAIN THEM.

The only thing worse than not creating a good relationship at all is creating a connection with customers that they can't rely on. When a service provider seems interested initially but doesn't maintain the relationship after the sale, the customer feels manipulated. It's almost like a bait and switch.

If you are in sales, you know the importance of keeping the connections you create, even if the prospect didn't buy from you. Not only is it good business to follow up and say thank you after you make the sale, it can also be good business to follow up with those who *didn't* buy to say, "Thanks for considering our products, and please let me know if I can ever help you in the future."

2. IT DOESN'T HAVE TO TAKE MUCH TIME.

Sometimes going above and beyond requires a significant investment of time and effort. But in general, those who relate well to others don't spend extra hours each day relating. It isn't about how much time you spend with those in a professional setting (although that is important) but how quickly and authentically you are able to demonstrate your concern and commitment. Being fully present when engaging with others is effective and doesn't have to take much extra time. It simply involves putting aside any distractions and giving the person you are with your undivided attention.

3. FRIENDLINESS IS A CHOICE, NOT A RESPONSE.

It's easy to be friendly to nice people, but how do you deal with angry customers? If you depend on the mood of the other person, you'll be limited in who you can connect with. The test of friendliness is the ability to be pleasant to someone who is being unpleasant to you. Instead of fighting fire with fire, try responding to negativity with positivity. It may not change the other person, but it will keep him or her from changing you.

4. EMPLOYEES RARELY TREAT CUSTOMERS BETTER THAN THEIR EMPLOYER TREATS THEM.

One of the biggest complaints I get from employees is that their manager wants them to be nice to customers even though the manager isn't nice to them.

Treating employees differently than you expect them to treat customers is shortsighted, if not delusional. You communicate more powerfully with your behavior than you do with your words. Unfortunately, just as good behavior can be paid forward, poor behavior can be passed on as well. As Eleanor Roosevelt said, "It is not fair to ask of others what you are not willing to do yourself."

5. NICE ISN'T ENOUGH IF YOU'RE NOT COMPETENT.

If you're about to undergo surgery, your first concern is that your surgeon is competent and capable. All the niceness in the world is no substitute if the doctor is a hack.

Once the competency expectation is met, a relationship is the icing on the cake. A doctor who is competent *and* who makes the time to take a personal interest, communicate clearly, and express empathy will have a far larger and more committed patient base than a doctor who is merely good at what he or she does. On the flip side, studies show that the number one factor in malpractice suits is a breakdown in doctor-patient communication.

Relationship is important, but make sure you're offering a good product and good service first.

6. RELATIONSHIPS AREN'T BUILT IN A DAY.

Many people in the marketplace seem to have "Relationship ADD"—they expect instant payback from customers, and when they don't get it, they lose interest and abandon the customer altogether.

We build relationships over time by giving those we interact with our consistent and undivided attention. I worked for a sales organization where the sales manager told us, "Sell 'em and forget 'em. You don't have time to get to know customers." With such a mismatch in values, I knew my time there would be short. And as it turned out, the sales manager didn't stay long either.

FIVE SURPRISING WORDS FOR BUILDING BETTER RELATIONSHIPS

Building better relationships takes effort, but it isn't really that complicated. Here are a few key words to remember as you pursue connections with people at work and at home.

1. LOVE

The writer William George Jordan once said, "Love can transmute all duties into privileges, all responsibilities into joys."

When I was writing *The Fred Factor*, I got some editorial feedback steering me away from using the word *love*. The concern was that the word *love* "freaks businesspeople out," and my critic suggested safer but—to my way of thinking—far less accurate synonyms.

It may be true that the word *love* freaks some people out in a business context, especially when they think of it in terms of romance or sugary-sweet sentiment. But it is undeniable that the most effective people I've met imbue their work with love. They don't always talk about their work or those they serve in those terms, but their love is evident in their actions.

Love in work clothes is about treating people with dignity and respect. The real test of love is the ability to be kind and considerate to those who don't make it easy to do. I want to be careful to include a disclaimer here that nobody—whether in the home or workplace—should put up with abuse of any kind. I'm not talking here about abusers or situations where you might need to draw boundaries.

I'm talking about extending love to those who can be prickly, unhappy, or indifferent. We can't always win such people over, but we can refuse to respond in kind to their negativity.

2. REDEMPTION

Redemption isn't a word you hear much in business, but it can transform relationships. It is about recovering something that was lost at some cost to yourself—whether through your actions, words, or money.

When I was speaking at a large convention in Las Vegas, I was in a hurry to get to my mic check. The hotel had security checking badges outside the meeting area.

The security guy stopped me. "Where's your badge?"

"I'm a speaker for the meeting," I explained. "I'm on my way to the sound check."

My words were met with a blank expression. "You still need a badge."

Great, I thought. *This is just what I need.* "I really need to get to my room."

"Then you really need a badge," he responded.

My frustration turned to irritation. "Fine. I'll go all the way back to the registration desk to get my badge." Then I added something that I was sure he'd heard before. "And what is *your* name?"

This, of course, suggested he might be in big trouble for sending me back.

"My name is Joel," he said. "Make sure you tell them what a good job I'm doing providing security."

I had to admit that this made me smile. Joel was playing it by the book, but he also had a dry sense of humor. I got my badge and returned to see Joel, but I'm sure I wasn't exuding warm fuzzy feelings when I finally gained access. This was an inconvenient situation made worse by my bad attitude. After all, Joel had been hired to check badges. In his work, he'd no doubt heard every excuse. But his job was to make sure everybody had the right credentials.

> **"Love is willing the ultimate good for the other person."**
> —Fred Smith

After my mic check, I walked back to find Joel still at his station. I extended my hand. "Joel, I'm sorry for being a jerk," I said. "You are doing a good job, and I apologize."

He shook my hand and accepted my apology.

I can't tell for sure, but I think he appreciated the gesture. And I sure felt better. I couldn't undo my poor reaction, but I could redeem the situation—and the relationship.

3. MERCY

Mercy means not giving people what they deserve when they fall short of your expectations. It's also about giving them the benefit of the doubt—or cutting them some slack, to use a technical term.

If you blow your horn at an irritating driver, what happens when he looks into the rearview mirror and you realize you know him? If you're like most drivers, your attitude instantly changes. Instead of waving your fist, you wave a cheerful greeting.

"Hey, Bob, good to see you!" You hope he thinks you were honking to get his attention.

Here's the point: he was still driving poorly. Nothing about him changed, but something important about *you* changed: your perspective.

Why is it that we're so quick to give ourselves the benefit of the doubt but so slow to do so for others? My wife, Darla, is good at reminding me that there well could be extenuating circumstances causing others to do things that I too quickly label as annoying or wrong. And as much as I hate to admit it, she is absolutely right.

Why is it that we're so quick to give ourselves the benefit of the doubt but so slow to do so for others?

We give our friends the benefit of the doubt because we know them. If we want to be better at building relationships, we should assume the best about others and extend the benefit of the doubt before we know them. That greatly will increase the likelihood that they'll become our friends—or at least recognize that we are friendly.

A free pass or a "get out of jail free" card says as much about the nature of the mercy giver as the mercy getter.

4. GRACE

Grace is about giving people what they don't deserve—extending unmerited favor. If we all got exactly what we deserved and only what we deserved, most of us would not be where we are today.

Think of all the times that someone—a parent, a friend, a coworker, or even a Good Samaritan—extended a kindness to you that you didn't earn.

If you approach others with the attitude that you will only give them as much as they give to you, your relationship never will have a chance to grow beyond that point. But when someone makes a gesture based on grace—a gift or good deed that is unearned or undeserved—the relationship is deepened and enriched for both parties.

A gift given in grace will delight the one who receives it, as well as the one who gives it. Grace is one of the deepest forms of communication in any relationship. It says you care about someone for who that person is, not just what he or she does for you.

Fred once shared with me, "Many people will never know what I did for them, and that's okay. I didn't do it so they'd know. I did it because I wanted to be of service." He was willing to extend grace because his motivation was giving service, not just getting recognition.

5. COMPASSION

Compassion isn't just a feeling of deep sympathy and sorrow for another person who is stricken by misfortune; it is a feeling that is also accompanied by a strong desire to alleviate the suffering.

Stephanie Ponti, who runs a CPR training firm in California, shared a wonderful story of compassion with me.

When we were returning home from a training course, we didn't know that our gas gauge wasn't working.

Our vehicle ran out of gas in a very remote area. It was getting dark, it was cold, and we were twenty miles from anywhere.

After about an hour, an older-model van stopped, and the driver asked if we needed help. We explained our situation, and without letting us give him money, he took off to get us some gas.

As he was pulling away, I thanked him.

He yelled back, "No problem. My name is Hugo, and I work at the Marriott. Service is in my blood!"

About forty-five minutes later, Hugo returned. He parked so his headlights were on our vehicle, and he assisted in pouring the gas in the tank.

We thanked him and were soon off on our way.

It wasn't long before my son's cell phone started ringing. He had given our hero his number, and Hugo was calling to see if we were okay.

We told him yes, and he said, "Good. Now I can go to sleep and not worry about you guys!"

Stephanie said that brief experience of compassion—receiving service and care in a time of need—profoundly affected her family and her work.

Love, *redemption*, *mercy*, *grace*, and *compassion* aren't words that typically would come to mind when you think about building better, deeper business relationships. They're extraordinary concepts, and that's why they make for extraordinary relationships.

As we work on building better relationships, it's vital to understand that relationships are works in progress. They are living things. Strong relationships require significant attention if they're going to grow and deepen, but the time and effort put into them almost always pay dividends.

··

A SECOND LOOK

Think about these keys to building better relationships:

love

redemption

mercy

grace

compassion

Which of these words are the most challenging for you? Think about someone at work or at home you'd like to build a stronger relationship with. How can you demonstrate one of these qualities to him or her this week?

CHAPTER 9

ELEVATE THE EXPERIENCE

We see our customers as invited guests to a party, and we
are the hosts. It's our job every day to make every important
aspect of the customer experience a little bit better.

JEFF BEZOS

DOING THINGS the Fred way creates a different kind of experience for the people you meet, work with, and serve. It's what I like to call an "elevated experience."

An elevated experience happens when you are expecting something standard or run of the mill and you end up with something more. That's what happened when I met Fred. I was expecting an ordinary postman who shoved mail into my box. Instead, I found a difference maker who genuinely cared. I haven't stopped talking about him since!

Jennifer Griffith is the president of Commerce National Bank in Columbus, Ohio. When we worked together at an event, she shared this story of a Fred she encountered.

> **An elevated experience happens when you are expecting something standard or run of the mill and you end up with something more.**

I was having a relatively rushed start to my day. Commerce was hosting an Economic Forecast breakfast, and I needed to cut out early to try to make a grumpy customer in Cincinnati (about one hundred miles away) happy again.

About twenty minutes or so into my drive, I popped a tire. It wasn't until then that I realized I had forgotten to charge my phone. All I had left was one measly bar of battery juice, which easily could have been lost to 1-800-I-Need-a-Tow-Truck. Likewise, if I tried to please my grumpy client by phone, I was certain the call would be dropped when the battery died, and he'd be even more frustrated. I needed to get to Cincinnati on time, and I was at a momentary loss of how to get this done.

Then it came to me: *Of course! Call Kevin!*

Kevin King is the general manager at Byers Imports and has sold me, my husband, and my mother several cars. We were introduced by a common friend and client and have been sharing business ever since. I knew Kevin wouldn't let me down, and even if he was busy, he has a remarkable team that was certain to help.

Kevin heard my plea for help, asked me for my mile marker, and instructed me to stay put. Moments later, Kevin personally arrived with a vehicle to get me to Cincinnati, a hot cup of coffee, and a phone charger! I left my car in Kevin's care and jumped back on the road. I made my appointment on time, accepted several calls with my fully charged phone, and managed to have a stress-free day.

The following day I called Byers to arrange to pick up my car and return the gift they'd let me drive. To my surprise, I learned that with my last oil change, they had added a tire warranty, and there was no charge on the tire replacement. Things kept getting better! And they wouldn't dream of making me drive to them—they brought my car to my office. If I would just leave the keys to the car I had borrowed at the front desk, they would handle the rest.

My car was returned promptly, and I was glowing with appreciation. As Kevin was driving away, I received his text message: "By the way, we washed your floor mats. They are drying in the trunk."

When I thanked Kevin for the extraordinary experience he provided, I couldn't help adding, "But when you washed the floor mats, you were showing off!"

Buying a car can be a tedious event or a memorable experience. What I love about this story is that Kevin created a superior experience *after* the sale—and in unexpected ways.

When asked about why he does these things that are beyond the call of duty, Kevin said, "I've asked my team to go the extra mile because it matters and it creates loyalty in ways that advertising never will."

THE FOUR-WAY TEST OF AN ELEVATED EXPERIENCE

Jennifer's experience with Kevin touches on the four elements of an elevated experience. You can use these principles to elevate the experiences of your own customers and clients.

1. THEY ARE SURPRISED—IN A GOOD WAY.

Nobody likes a bad surprise like getting a flat tire. But Jennifer's angst turned to happiness when Kevin came to her rescue.

It wouldn't have been unreasonable for Kevin to suggest that Jennifer call AAA or roadside assistance. But as Kevin recognized, a problem is an opportunity to increase loyalty, if it's handled correctly. Kevin provided a level of service that far exceeded Jennifer's expectations.

Do your customers feel pleasantly surprised by the level of service you provide?

2. THEY ARE HAPPIER AFTER THE EXPERIENCE THAN THEY WERE BEFORE.

Even having a problem can make you happier in the end if the problem is resolved satisfactorily. In this case, Jennifer was impressed—perhaps even astounded—at the lengths Kevin was willing to go to help.

Think about the happiness level of your customers before their interactions with you and after. Do they feel better because of the experience you created?

3. THEY FEEL THEY'VE RECEIVED VALUE.

At its core, value refers to the informed feelings you have. If customers have received value, they feel they got what they paid for—or more. If they got a good deal but they don't feel that way, well, sorry—it wasn't value.

Here's what's interesting about Jennifer's story: she had already purchased her car and received value for what she paid. When Kevin responded in an extraordinary way to her post-purchase dilemma—a situation that was in no way his fault—she received additional value for doing business with Byers Imports. That additional value will guarantee that Jennifer keeps going back.

4. THEY WANT TO TELL OTHERS ABOUT THEIR EXPERIENCE.

Jennifer loves to tell this story and was delighted to share it with me. I, in turn, am sharing it with you. An elevated experience creates "brand evangelists"—customers who will go to their peers and sing your praises. This kind of buzz is better than any advertising Byers might invest in. And who knows? If you live in the Columbus area, you might already be thinking about buying your next car at Byers. That's the power of an elevated experience.

YOU'VE JUST GOT TO C.A.R.E.

Sadly, the elevated experience is all too rare. But that doesn't have to be the case for you—it's not that hard to make a memorable opportunity for those you serve. The best proof of your commitment to customers is to C.A.R.E.: Create A Rare Experience.

Here are eight ways to elevate the experiences you provide and to really C.A.R.E.

1. ELIMINATE WORRY.

Any experience is better when you don't have to worry or fret about it.

In my years of observing the business world, I've come to define a professional as someone who is more worried about the solutions to your problems and needs than you are. A professional health care provider is more concerned about your health than you are. A professional educator is more worried about your education (or your child's education) than you are.

A professional is someone who is more worried about the solutions to your problems and needs than you are.

If you are willing to take on your customers' problems to reduce the worry in their lives, they'll reward you with loyalty.

To elevate the experience, reassure those you serve by taking out the worry.

2. BE INVOLVED BEFORE, DURING, AND AFTER.

A sale doesn't create a customer. Selling merely creates a transaction. What happens before and after the transaction determines whether you have a customer for life or a customer for that transaction only. Most businesses seem to wash their hands of their customers after a sale. By staying hands-on with your customers even after you already have their money, however, you will stand out as truly rare. Customers will notice, come back, and tell others.

Providing great service for a customer after a sale is one of the best ways to elevate the experience.

3. PAY ATTENTION TO DETAILS.

Sometimes the devil can be in the dust.

Recently a nice repairman worked on the fan in my bathroom. He was courteous and said he'd let me know when he could come back with the parts he needed to fix the fan. After he left, I noticed dust floating down from the now fanless vent covering. He had removed and reinstalled the covering without getting rid of the accumulated dust. He had, however, dislodged enough of it to float down on my head.

Not a big deal, but a noticeable deal. This small negative difference could have been easily corrected by applying some simple common sense.

How often do we miss opportunities to remove the dust that irritates our customers, colleagues, and others?

My wife and I both have used the same facility to get MRIs. My trip was a delight: the staff was prompt, friendly, and professional. They kept candy and snacks available for patients, as well as soft drinks and coffee. There were TVs and current magazines in the waiting room. I was pleased.

Several weeks later, I took my wife to the same office for her MRI. Since someone on the phone had told her to arrive by 6:30, we made sure to be on time. After waiting for fifty minutes, I was no longer happy, even with candy and coffee. I inquired as to the reason for the wait.

I received the following curt response: "You came early. You weren't supposed to check in until seven o'clock."

Many of the good feelings about my past experience were undone by one important detail: someone on the phone had given my wife the wrong arrival time.

Despite our best intentions to provide something extra or something elevated, if we don't attend to details, all our efforts will be wasted when the customer gets something less than he or she expected.

4. INVOLVE OTHERS APPROPRIATELY.

On a trip to Israel with a hundred members from our church, my wife, Darla, and I were on one of three tour buses with a guide named Shimone. He was a talented guide, had a great sense of humor, and was a master at involving the group with pop quizzes and riddles.

One of the important logistical matters on the trip was making sure everyone boarded the bus before we left a site. Shimone could have done that himself or delegated the job to the bus driver, but he did one better. Pat, a member of our group who was traveling alone on the trip, was a thoughtful and gregarious guy, always willing to do whatever he could to help. Shimone decided to put him in charge.

"You will all check in with Mr. Pat," Shimone said. "He has agreed to keep track of you. He'll always make sure everyone stays together."

To someone other than "Mr. Pat," this assignment might have been a burden, but it was an ideal fit for his personality. Not only was he delighted to help, but we were also glad to be shepherded by him. Pat's experience was elevated by his involvement, and so was everyone else's.

How can you involve others in the experience in ways they'll appreciate?

5. FABRICATE FUN.

Fun is serious business. That's why people love the wizardry of Chuck E. Cheese's, IMAX theaters, theme parks, and other entertainment experiences.

People love to be entertained.

Entertainment really elevates the experience when it happens in a nontraditional environment. The attendants at

Southwest Airlines are known for joking or even singing their way through the preflight instructions. Some are so entertaining that passengers have posted videos of them on YouTube. Talk about free advertising and brand evangelism!

What can you do to add unexpected entertainment to the service you provide?

6. LOOK FOR PROBLEMS TO SOLVE.

Airports offer an experience, but typically it's not an enjoyable one. Often I've wondered why there aren't seats in the pickup area for people who are waiting for a ride. Maybe airports don't want people sitting around waiting, but they have to wait regardless, and it would be nice if they had a place to sit.

This less-than-ideal airport experience could explain why many airport lounges have recently gotten upgrades. People can use these lounges to relax or get work done. Airlines say that better lounges attract more premium ticket sales. Some amenities, such as work stations, free Wi-Fi, computers, printers, and fax machines, can be accessed through the loyalty program. Some airlines, like Virgin, even offer personal assistants and services like massages, hair styling, and manicures.

Are there some simple measures that would elevate your customers' experiences? Are there problems your customers are facing that could be solved easily? Often an elevated experience can be provided by solving simple problems that no one else has identified. Be the first to find them.

7. OFFER ADDED INFORMATION.

My friend Taylor Scott tells about his experience at Disney California Adventure, an experience-rich environment if ever there was one.

While he and his friend Sonny were visiting, they met Carlos, a merchandise cast member.

"Are you guys having fun?" Carlos asked. "Is this your first time here?"

Taylor explained that he and Sonny were big fans with lots of experience at the park.

"Well then, do you know the secret to spicing up our most popular attractions? Let me give you a couple of tips. When you go on the Tower of Terror, make sure you sit in the middle row—row 5, I believe it is—and sit in the very middle seats in that row. As you go up in the elevator car, just before it drops, pick up your feet and raise your knees up toward your chest. You'll fly right out of the seat, and it's just an unbelievable ride. Try it. You'll love it!"

Taylor and Sonny took his advice, and they did love it. They both agreed that after riding on multimillion-dollar attractions, seeing fantastic theatrical performances, and being immersed in the magic of Disney, what stood out most was Carlos.

"We couldn't stop talking about Carlos and how he created a moment, an experience, and truly made a positive difference out of thin air."

And it didn't cost a penny!

That's what Freds do. They create value simply by using their ingenuity and personality.

You probably know more about your business than your customers do. Sharing a little inside information will elevate their experience, as well as their opinion of you and your company.

8. ANTICIPATE YOUR CUSTOMERS' NEEDS.

I never cease to be amazed at the greeting I receive when I enter a hotel with my bags in tow. "Checking in?" the employee at the front desk asks.

I'm always tempted to say, "No, I'm just walking my luggage."

The best way to greet a customer is with the question, how may I help you? If no assistance is needed, the customer will let you know. But you really elevate the experience when you think ahead and anticipate what the customer might need.

When Kevin "rescued" Jennifer from her flat tire and dying phone, he also brought her a cup of coffee because he knew she drank it and that, after a challenging morning, she just might need a little more energy.

The best Freds anticipate needs and solve problems in advance. Most of the time those needs are easy to foresee. Just put yourself in your customers' shoes and imagine what would elevate their experience. That's how you C.A.R.E.

A SIDE OF HUGS

Jim Morris is a believer in the Fred principles, so his antennae are always up for Fred sightings. He met a friend for lunch at Ivey's, a restaurant in Madison, Alabama. He'd been hearing a lot about it from other customers, and after his first visit he understood why the business was doing well.

Ivey's specializes in home-cooked Southern foods like chicken, pork chops, and roast, as well as incredible desserts. What makes Ivey's special, Jim learned, is the owner/manager, Ms. Swanner.

"I noticed Ms. Swanner soon after we'd taken our seats," Jim said. "She was wearing a red apron and was giving patrons a small bowl of her homemade banana pudding, along with a little something extra: a hug."

When she made it to Jim's table, she introduced herself and thanked him for dining at her establishment. She also made Jim get out of his seat to give her a hug, which he did gladly. After a delicious meal of pork chops and green beans, Jim decided to pass on dessert. Not so fast. Ms. Swanner made her way back to his table.

"If you're not going to order dessert, you at least need to have a few bites." She brought over a generous serving of banana pudding, on the house.

"My friend and I couldn't escape the presence of this great lady. We went in expecting great food, and we left with the feeling that we had been in the presence of an angel," he said.

As Jim was leaving the restaurant, Ms. Swanner poked her head out the door and said, "Jim, are you going home? 'Cause if you are, you need to take some of this banana pudding to your kids."

Wow, he thought. *Not only did she remember my name, but she remembered that I'd told her about my kids.*

When Jim wrote about his experience in a blog post, he added, "For all of you *Fred Factor* fans, Ms. Swanner is definitely a Fred."

Providing an elevated experience is what Freds do. We've come to expect the minimum from most of our service experiences. When a Fred offers an unexpected extra, it makes a difference, builds relationships, and creates value.

As rare as they are, elevated experiences aren't that difficult to create. When you elevate the experiences of those around you, you create loyal customers who feel cared about—and will sing your praises to others too.

TAKE TIME TO C.A.R.E.

Identify one of your key customers or clients. Write out three simple things you could do for that customer to create a rare experience the next time you provide a service for him or her.

Customer: Action:

CHAPTER 10

RENEW YOUR RESOLVE

It is easy to deliver extraordinary results—once. Making that part of your everyday process is difficult. The really tough thing is when your customers (patients, in my case) begin to expect that high level of customer service and you have to clear that higher bar.

MATT MESSINA, DDS

THREE OF THE SADDEST words I know are "I used to . . ."

I frequently encounter people who tell me they used to practice the Fred philosophy. They used to be of service in the community. They were once committed to excellent service. But not anymore.

What happened?

The common explanation is they lost their passion and enthusiasm. They got tired, burned out, or discouraged. The challenges of life overcame their commitment, and they lost heart.

Chapter 4 talks about the importance of starting with commitment. But that isn't enough. If you truly desire to be extraordinary, you have to keep your commitment vital and ongoing. It may be time to renew your resolve.

STAYING THE SAME JUST ISN'T ENOUGH

So many individuals and organizations achieve excellence and erroneously think that's the final destination. Success, however it's defined, is a moving target. Staying the same isn't enough because yesterday's success can easily become tomorrow's mediocrity.

In fact, success usually gives rise to more challenges and competition. Why is that? For one thing, it gives your customers and coworkers rising expectations. The downside of doing a good job is that people come to expect an even better job next time. Also, competitors will keep offering your customers more in an effort to win their business from you. They'll be watching what you do and, if they're clever, trying to one-up you.

You will always have new challenges to contend with. Those include not only outside forces like competitors and adverse economic conditions but also new policies and processes within your organization. What worked in the past can be thwarted by new developments.

Staying the same isn't enough because yesterday's success can easily become tomorrow's mediocrity.

On a personal level, staying the same doesn't challenge you. After all, once you've figured something out, what's left to do? You need to continually aim to raise your game if you're going to keep your energy and enthusiasm going.

College football coach Nick Saban, who has coached teams to three national championships, says that how we deal with success is a better indicator of character than how we deal with failure.

"I think the most difficult thing in life in terms of being

successful is consistency in performance, especially when you have success," Saban says. "Most people deal with failure pretty decently—it motivates them; they want to do better. But when they have success, they tend to feel a little entitled and think, *I met my quota for this month, so I should get a little time off.*"

With this in mind, we need to be intentional about keeping our commitment solid and our enthusiasm strong. Here are some ways to renew our resolve.

1. DECIDE TO BE HAPPY HERE AND NOW.

According to speaker and author Charlie "Tremendous" Jones, "If you can't be happy where you are, it's a cinch you can't be happy where you ain't."

I've never met an unhappy Fred. I'm sure Freds have times when they're unhappy—we all do—but I've never met a consistently sour Fred. That demeanor just doesn't go with the spirit of Fred. The truth is, if you're not basically happy, you'll have a hard time spreading happiness to others. You can't give what you don't have.

Science backs up what Freds inherently know—Freds not only live better; they also live longer. A thirty-year study by Mayo Clinic found that optimists live longer than pessimists. It turns out that looking on the bright side and letting go of things you can't control is good for your health!

We all have our lot in life (and sometimes it feels like a used car lot to me!). Life isn't easy. But often it's simpler than we make it. We have a choice: we can change our lot or we can accept it. If we aren't able to change our lot in life, despite our best efforts, we're down to one option: accept it.

But the way we accept it makes all the difference. We can

expend our energy kicking and screaming against the injustice of our situation, or we can accept with grace and magnanimity the conditions we can't control. Freds, I've come to believe, go one step beyond. They don't just change their lot in life; they help others live on a better lot too.

2. TRY SOMETHING DIFFERENT.

Are you employed where you really want to work? If not, what steps are you taking to find more meaningful and rewarding work?

While it's wise to find a career that's a good fit for you, don't make the mistake of thinking a different environment is necessarily going to solve all your problems. People often think they will be happy if they could just find a different job. However, I've observed that unhappiness tends to follow people. If you aren't happy now, a different job probably won't make you happy either. A better alternative might be to do your current job differently.

Have you ever seen a police officer wearing earphones while directing traffic and having his or her own private dance session, waving arms and tooting a whistle? It's enjoyable for motorists to observe, but more than that, I have to believe it makes directing traffic a lot more fun for the police officer too.

An ordinary employee might think that the job of directing traffic is drudgery. But a Fred thinks, *I'm doing the work I've been given to do here, so why not make the most of it?*

I shared this story when I was speaking recently, and an audience member approached me afterward.

"I directed a lot of traffic in the aftermath of Hurricane Katrina," he said. "It was really stressful. People were angry and on edge. But a funny thing happened. When we started having fun directing traffic—being more patient and engaging motorists in a positive way—they responded in kind. They offered us food, told us jokes, and conversed with us. It made the situation better all the way around."

Helen Keller said that life is either a daring adventure or nothing. There is satisfaction in knowing that you do extraordinary work simply by choice. It is also gratifying to be extraordinary for the sake of others who are facing trials. You have the opportunity to make their journeys a little more enjoyable, and along the way you'll find that your journey improves as well.

You can suffer through your work, or you can surf through the day, adding as much happiness and fun as you possibly can. Nobody can make that choice but you.

3. REMIND YOURSELF REGULARLY.

Remembering to make doctor's appointments, pick up milk on the way home, return those DVDs, and get your oil changed takes up lots of memory. By now you have probably developed different ways to remember those important things you're supposed to do.

Sometimes when we're making life changes, our biggest challenge is remembering to carry out the decisions we've made. It isn't that we're not committed to taking this step to do something new or implement something better. It just takes a lot less energy to do things the same way we've always done them.

The same phenomenon applies to being a Fred. Even if you agree with the Fred philosophy and want to resemble Fred in spirit and behavior, your good intentions will fail if you don't first remember what to do.

Here are five easy ways to remind yourself to be a Fred.

- Stamp it into your memory—literally.

  Since the original Fred is a postman, what better reminder than a postage stamp? You could stick a postage stamp to your calendar, on your computer, somewhere in your car, or even on your bathroom mirror. Each time you see the stamp, you'll be reminded of your commitment to being a Fred. You'll be on the lookout for more opportunities to serve and to improve what you provide.

- Let Fred become music to your ears.

  Choose a song you like—one you hear often—and use it as a trigger. Each time you hear that song, think about the Fred opportunities in front of you, the Freds you've seen recently, and how you can be like Fred throughout your day.

- Learn from the Freds of the past.

  A great way to renew your commitment to being a Fred is to post quotes where you'll see them and read them often. Over time your mind will be transformed by the ideas. These quotes will become part of how you think and speak. For example, you might post a quote like this one by Nobel Laureate Albert Schweitzer: "Constant kindness can accomplish much. As the sun makes ice melt, kindness causes misunderstanding, mistrust, and hostility to evaporate."

- Recognize the Freds you encounter each day.

  Recognizing others for doing the kinds of things you want to do is an effective way to integrate the ideas into your own life. When you take time to thank and appreciate the Freds around you, that in itself is acting on the Fred philosophy.

- Review regularly.
    Once a month, make an appointment with yourself to review the Fred principles. Making any meaningful change requires diligence, awareness, and conscious effort. It helps to be periodically reminded of and inspired by Fred.

The best way to be a Fred—and help create that spirit and attitude in others—is first by remembering and then by doing.

4. RETHINK YOUR PERSPECTIVE.

Take some time for reflection. Are you living by your values? Are you happy and successful? Are you productive or just busy?

Pessimism goes much deeper than just seeing the glass as half-empty. It is tied to this underlying fear: not only is the glass half-empty, but it has no hope of getting a refill. The combination of pessimism and a scarcity mind-set virtually guarantees a losing outcome for everyone involved.

If we go through life thinking that every little effort will sap the lifeblood out of us or that we'll never recover the extra energy we spend on creative service, we will be bound by the limitations we

Pessimism is tied to this underlying fear: not only is the glass half-empty, but it has no hope of getting a refill.

have set. We'll hunker down, conserving every bit of energy we have as if it's the last we'll ever possess. We'll find ourselves scrambling to protect what little we think we have and ultimately doing only what is essential for survival.

In contrast, if we believe we have what we need to exceed others' expectations without draining our own resources to dangerously low levels, we are free to take action. In the process of serving, we find ourselves energized and fulfilled.

If the original Fred had operated merely from a survival perspective, he would have delivered the mail as quickly as possible, avoided contact with the people on his route, and scoffed at the idea he could provide more. If he had bought into that mind-set, there wouldn't have been a Fred to write about—or at the very least, I would have been talking about someone with a different name.

But Fred understood some things about the way the world works, and that gave him the needed perspective to go the extra mile.

- Fred realized that it takes very little—and sometimes no—additional time to do an extraordinary job instead of an adequate job.
- He realized that being friendly doesn't drain your energy; in fact, usually it boosts your energy.
- He realized that providing excellent service rather than ordinary service requires only a little desire and creativity.

Much like flipping a switch, moving from a pessimistic outlook to an optimistic one will have an immediate effect on your ability to be a Fred. The difference is like a room when the light is turned on: it is the same room, but the light makes it look different. This mind-set goes much deeper than seeing the glass as half-full. It recognizes that even if the glass isn't full now, it quickly could be filled to overflowing. With that sort of reassurance, Freds know they have the power, energy, and resources to make a difference in the lives of people around them.

5. REWARD YOURSELF.

Every day do two things: something challenging and something fun. One will make you better, and the other will make you happier. When you accomplish something, find a way to pat yourself on the back. When you reach a goal, throw yourself a little party.

Hard work, commitment, and dedication are the stuff of resolve. But as the saying goes, "All work and no play makes Jack a dull boy." Choose some benchmarks and attainable goals, and then create a list of small, doable rewards (such as going for a ten-minute walk, buying your favorite coffee drink, calling a friend, or doing anything else that is positive and enjoyable for you). When you get to each finish line, pick a prize from the list. Don't cheat on your goals, but don't cheat yourself, either. When you've done something well, you deserve to celebrate the accomplishment.

6. TAKE TIME TO REST.

Renewing your resolve can help you keep your nose to the grindstone when you need to. But you can't keep your nose to the grindstone for long periods of time without breaks or you will lose both your nose and your resolve. Rest is a critical ingredient for both happiness and productivity. Henry

Ford understood this and argued for a forty-hour workweek that would allow workers evenings and weekends. He knew that his workers would be less productive without sufficient rest.

Getting a good night's sleep is important to your mental and physical health, as well as to your productivity. Likewise, studies have shown that short naps make people more productive and alert. It's also important to realize that some rest doesn't come in the form of sleep. Take the time to relax with a movie or book or go to the beach or park or simply do some thinking and daydreaming. Remember: no rest, no resolve.

YOU CAN DENT THE UNIVERSE

We all start the day the same way: with terrible breath and funky hair. My guess is that you don't look in the mirror first thing in the morning and say, "Today I'm going to change the world!" Sounds a bit melodramatic, doesn't it?

Yet we do change the world in various ways for the people we come in contact with each day. It's up to us whether that change will be positive or negative. I like the way Steve Jobs put it—that we're here to put a dent in the universe. Jobs and Apple certainly made a big dent with their ideas and technology. You and I may not be creating the next world-changing technology, but we can make our own dents.

When you implement these strategies into your daily life, good things start to happen. The magic happens when you combine solid, usable ideas into a philosophy that gradually becomes a guide for you and those you work with.

There is no magic formula, but there is magic *in* the formula.

KEEP IT FRESH

Here are a few tangible ways to renew your resolve and keep the Fred philosophy at the forefront of your mind.

1. Acknowledge other Freds. A great way to recognize the Freds you encounter is with the Fred Factor Recognition Certificate—signed by Mark Sanborn and Fred the Postman himself. You can order a downloadable version at The Mark Sanborn Store, www.marksanborn.com/store.

2. Review the Fred principles. If you'd like a quick, easy way to review the Fred principles, you can order Fred Factor Principles Summary Cards. They are available at The Mark Sanborn Store, www.marksanborn.com/store.

3. Choose a quote that reflects your values and print it out. Post it somewhere you'll see it as a tangible reminder of the way you want to live and do business.

CHAPTER 11

WHAT IF YOU'RE A HEAD FRED?

*The secret to success is good leadership, and good leadership is all about
making the lives of your team members or workers better.*
TONY DUNGY

THE FIRST JOB of leadership is to help people see their significance. Leaders recognize that those who feel insignificant rarely make significant contributions. An effective leader is able to show people that they are significant in ways they may not realize.

After I shared this principle at an event, I heard from an audience member who explained that he had served in the Air National Guard. A commanding officer was visiting his unit and asked one of the men what he did for ANG.

The man replied, "I'm just a cook, sir."

The commanding officer bellowed back, "Just a cook? Sir, do you know what that means?"

The cook was a bit taken aback, but he certainly was listening.

The officer continued, "You, sir, provide meals and nutrition for the men and women who support our pilots. Those men and women service the airplanes and support the pilots who provide defense for our nation. Those who eat the food you prepare drive trucks, handle armaments, and support ground troops. Their ability to do their jobs, and do them well, depends on how well fed they are. Nourishment is an essential element of success that is often taken for granted—but should never be."

The officer looked squarely at the cook. "You, sir, are a cook, but you are not merely a cook. You are a warrior who contributes to the best and highest purposes of the Air National Guard!"

The man who told me the story added, "It was the single most important story I remember from my experiences in the ANG all these years later."

A leader has the unique power to instill a sense of significance in others.

In this age of spin and hyperbole, some people think leadership is about telling a better story. And while leaders need to be effective communicators and storytellers, it is more important that they be effective story changers. Leaders don't just tell a better story; they make the story better.

Leaders don't just tell a better story; they make the story better.

The real test of leadership is this: is anyone or anything better because of you? Leadership is, in large part, a battle against mediocrity. Leaders pursue excellence, and that means ridding their teams and organizations of the triviality and poor performance that threatens any group.

Once you've created systems and processes to support the delivery of the extraordinary, you need to unleash the power of *who*. (Remember, the why is always a who.)

That means it's not enough to be a Fred yourself; you also need to develop and lead other Freds.

HOW TO LEAD FREDS

Wouldn't you like more of your coworkers and employees to be like Fred Shea? Think of the benefits of having team members who are committed to turning ordinary work into extraordinary work. That doesn't mean you want clones of Fred; you just need other people who embrace and exemplify his spirit.

Here are ten things you need to do to be a head Fred.

1. LEAD BY EXAMPLE.

The best way to have more Freds within your organization is to first be a Fred yourself. Fred-like behavior isn't something you can command or demand. Instead, you must be willing to model what that behavior looks like in your own performance—not only in how you treat customers but also in how you treat your employees and colleagues. Commit to working at a higher level, not because you have to but because you choose to.

I asked Fred about the importance of leading by example. He said, "You've got to model it first. If you don't, you have no business preaching it to others."

2. START WITH WHAT'S RIGHT INSTEAD OF WHAT'S WRONG.

Gratefulness creates a great fullness of heart. But you can't be grateful if you're focusing primarily on what's wrong and who's responsible. Start with "What's right?" and "Who is doing great work?" That doesn't mean you shouldn't address low performers or problems—just don't begin with them.

It may be tempting for a leader to say, "I don't have to worry about the people who are succeeding, so I'll just let them do their thing." But it's risky to ignore good performers and give all your attention to those who are underperforming. If you only grease the squeaky wheels, eventually all the wheels will start squeaking (or the nonsqueaky wheels will go elsewhere).

When you start with what's right and who is responsible, good things start happening:

- You give recognition where it's due.
- You focus the rest of the team on a positive example.
- You feel better about your role as the head Fred. This isn't self-deception; this is a legitimate way to count your blessings.

3. ENCOURAGE PEOPLE TO TRY.

You don't have to be great to start, but you have to start to be great.

Some people are afraid to try. They've attempted to act like Fred in the past, and either they weren't appreciated or they were reprimanded for an unsuccessful outcome. Other people have simply never tried to do anything out of the ordinary, perhaps because nobody expected or encouraged them to do so.

That's where you come in as a leader. You might need to prove your employees' own significance to them. Show them specifically where they can shine, and encourage them to try. Reward the attempt, not just the outcome. The only thing someone may need to get started on a journey toward greatness is a boost of support and encouragement from you.

4. ASK FOR AND SHARE IDEAS ABOUT HOW TO BE LIKE FRED.

The only thing better than a good idea is a good idea shared.

Regularly solicit examples and techniques from everyone on

your team about how to turn the ordinary into the extraordinary. Don't feel like you have to be the sole source of ideas. Get everyone involved in sharing better practices, and set aside times for people to talk about what they've done that has worked.

5. REMOVE BARRIERS AND OBSTACLES.

One of your goals as a leader is to make it as easy as possible for your team members to succeed. If you have protocols that hinder performance, either remove them or give people a free pass if they break them. As long as their behavior is moral and ethical, don't get hung up on needless policies and procedures.

Ask your Freds to fill in the blank in this statement: "The biggest barrier I have to performing better is _____." Pay attention to the specific problems they cite. Once you've identified the barriers and obstacles that stand in their way, you can work to remove those barriers.

6. BE THEIR CHAMPION.

Don't just try to be a hero—make heroes of those around you.

When your Freds do something noteworthy, tell everybody, including other departments. And make sure higher-ups in the company know. Ask the leaders in your firm to pen a note or send off an e-mail of appreciation to someone who delivered extraordinary service. If your team of Freds needs a particular resource, present that need to upper management. Use your influence with others within the organization to assist the Freds you lead.

7. GIVE THEM THE FREEDOM THEY NEED.

Don't treat everyone equally, or you'll create an organization of mediocrity. Treat everyone *fairly*, but make sure that those who perform best get appropriate preference. Performance should have its privileges.

Give high-performing Freds more latitude and freedom to do their work. The privilege of performance is a corollary to the idea that for those who are given much, much will be required. Those who contribute best and most should be considered for privileges not earned by ordinary performance.

Don't just expect more; recognize and reward more when you get it.

8. TEACH THE FRED PRINCIPLES CONSISTENTLY.

Repetition, it has been said, is the mother of retention. The four basic Fred principles are (1) everybody makes a difference; (2) it is all built on relationship; (3) you can add value to everything you do; and (4) you can reinvent yourself continually. Even when we have the best of intentions, the daily demands of a hectic workplace can push those values to the back burner.

That's why it's critical to consistently remind people about the principles and practices you want them to implement. Whenever something significant happens—whether good or bad—great teachers find a way to extract the important lessons. So look for the teachable moments.

When teaching the Fred principles, it pays to explain both *what* needs to be done and *why*. People are more motivated and committed when they're armed with reasons that make sense to them.

Part of teaching people includes giving them the training and tools they need to successfully meet the expectations. I can expect you to run a marathon, but if I don't offer the training and preparation you need, the odds are greatly diminished that you'll finish the race.

9. RECOGNIZE AND REWARD.

I have yet to meet someone who complained about being appreciated too much. And I rarely meet managers who are as good at appreciating their team as they could be. We all need to guard against this, especially since the longer we work with our colleagues, the more we tend to take them for granted.

Behavior that is rewarded tends to be repeated. That's all the more reason to put the spotlight on Fred-like behavior whenever you see it. You can use both formal and informal rewards when you see people acting like Freds. For example, you might recognize little successes with verbal praise and big accomplishments with larger tangible rewards. Consider giving employees note cards that say, "Thanks for being a Fred!" that they can pass on to those they appreciate within the organization.

When a customer tells you about something extraordinary one of your people has done, try to connect him or her with that person—by phone or in person—so the positive feedback will be more powerful and personal.

One word of caution, however: insincere or shallow recognition programs will fail. People don't want gratuitous praise. They want to be acknowledged for legitimate accomplishments. Cutesy or cursory attempts will waste your time and annoy employees.

10. ENJOY.

Someone recently asked how they could achieve Fred-like performance without creating added stress. If your attempts to encourage extraordinary performance are stressful, you're not doing something right. Freds don't work harder because they have to but because they want to. Leaders create "want to" in others.

When Fred goes on his route looking for ways to go beyond his duties, it adds joy, not stress, to his life. The process isn't stressful but enjoyable.

IT ISN'T ABOUT WHAT FRED SAYS

Many years ago, a leader invited me to work with his team. His organization was well respected and had an excellent reputation, and I appreciated his desire to keep improving. In all my conversations with him, he espoused a deep belief in and commitment to Fred-like ideals.

Midway through the seminar we stopped for a break. A small group of employees had gathered in the corner and were talking excitedly. My gut told me I needed to check in with them.

"How's it going?" I inquired.

There was a long pause. The group exchanged nervous glances.

Finally a brave woman spoke up. "We love what you're saying and really wish we saw more of those leadership behaviors here. But . . ." Another pause. "There is one person who seems to do the exact opposite of everything you're saying. And he's in a position of leadership."

I was justifiably concerned. I realized that I needed to keep whatever they shared confidential. "It is important for me to know who you're referring to. I won't share what you say with this person, but maybe I can help."

I was stunned when I learned the name of the offender: it was the man who had hired me.

I hadn't encountered that kind of mismatch between beliefs and behaviors before, and I never got to the bottom of what was causing the breakdown. The situation has, however, stayed with me as a warning.

Integrity is the distance between our lips and our lives. The most powerful prose and inspirational speaking will be of little use if we can't back them up with a life well lived, a life that demonstrates true leadership and the spirit of the extraordinary.

> **Integrity is the distance between our lips and our lives.**

To lead a team of Freds—to be a head Fred—you first need to be a Fred yourself. Your example will speak louder than your words. To be sure, you must communicate clearly with your team and share your ideals, goals, and values with them. But if you don't live them out yourself, your team won't embrace them either. Be who you say you are, and your team will become what you want them to be.

A TRUE HEAD FRED

I first met Court Durkalski when the two of us spoke at Southeastern University's Leadership Forum. We've since become friends, and over the years, I have been increasingly impressed with Court and the high standard of leadership he provides at Truline Industries, his tool and die company near Cleveland, Ohio.

What initially caught my attention was Court's comment

about encouraging employees to bring their problems to work. *Really? Did I hear that right?*

Here's how Court put it:

Employees today face many challenges. If they're married, there is a 50 percent chance they will experience a divorce. If they have a child, there is a 15 percent chance their child will battle an addiction to alcohol or drugs. There is a 30 percent chance their child has been bullied or is bullying someone else. Not to mention the death of friends and loved ones, a failing economy, or the pressure for success. It's no wonder the workforce is troubled and stressed.

Stress within the workplace is also prevalent due to continued downsizing and the constant pressure for higher profitability. Because of this, the average workplace is not a nurturing, caring environment.

As a result of seeing these problems, we had a vision many years ago to create a workplace in which employees were encouraged to "bring their problems to work." We believed employees had a need to feel loved, nurtured, and cared for and that their best chance for success was birthed in that type of culture.

People who are unencumbered by their problems or are in the process of successfully dealing with their problems have the greatest chance for high achievement. In the past two decades we have been successful in creating a corporate culture that functions more like a healthy family than a business, which, although not the goal, has also led to higher profitability.

One of our employees had a child who was born with serious birth defects. Doctors said the child would never progress mentally past the age of two. Then two years later, the employee was diagnosed with multiple sclerosis. During his tenure at Truline, we found ways to help him and his wife cope with their new reality. When his doctors determined it was a physical detriment for him to continue at Truline, we retained the services of a firm that specialized in long-term care for special needs children and adults. In the spirit of a family culture, Truline made a long-term financial commitment so his retirement would not be a financial burden.

We decided a long time ago that our actions must speak louder than our words. It's one thing to say we value our employees and quite another to show them. We want them to know we value them as people—even more than the function they may perform for the company.

Court Durkalski and Fred Shea know what it looks like to be a true head Fred—someone who leads by example and doesn't just talk about his or her values but acts on them. They recognize that sometimes there is a price for that commitment, but as Zig Ziglar reminds us, we can enjoy the price, not just pay it. As leaders' lives demonstrate, valuing people and helping them become the best they can be is what leadership is all about.

NEXT STEPS FOR A HEAD FRED

1. Consider implementing a training program around the Fred principles. Since there are four principles, it might work well to integrate a teaching or reinforcement session into a staff meeting once each quarter. (If you're looking for a ready-to-implement resource, *The Fred Factor DVD Training Curriculum* can be purchased from www.marksanborn.com/store.)

2. Find ways to share examples of Fred-like behavior you notice, both within and outside your organization. You might want to designate a bulletin board as a place where people can post these examples or e-mail them to your team.

3. Review some of the contributions your employees have made in the past that you didn't express adequate appreciation for at the time. Recall the situations and recognize them now to make up for the oversight.

CHAPTER 12

BUILD A TEAM FRED

*Never doubt that a small group of thoughtful, committed citizens can
change the world. Indeed, it is the only thing that ever has.*

MARGARET MEAD

"B-I-N-G-O" is a popular refrain from a traditional children's
melody about a farmer and his dog. But Cherry Crest Adventure
Farm in Lancaster County, Pennsylvania, has put a new twist on
the song, and it now spells customer service "F-R-E-D."

Cherry Crest Adventure Farm is an "agritainment" (agricul-
ture plus entertainment) facility with more than one hundred
thousand visitors annually. Organized around a corn maze,
Cherry Crest features more than fifty authentic farming attractions that keep families busy for hours.

While the employees at Cherry Crest know that first-rate
attractions are key to a successful operation, they also believe
superior customer service is an essential ingredient for attracting
returning customers. This is where Fred enters the farm scene.

Brian Waltman, the director of education, shared with me
his vision for creating a team of Freds at Cherry Crest. "I introduced the concept of Fred to the staff as a practical way of
fleshing out our customer service culture," he said.

Cherry Crest refers to their training process as "Fredification." The Fred concepts are clearly spelled out in the employee handbook, routinely visited in morning staff meetings, and reviewed in e-mail updates. Fred often shows up in daily conversations among staff members.

This past year Cherry Crest went one step further by incorporating the Fred idea into each person's annual performance review. Their revamped employee evaluation has all the typical elements, such as "meets job performance standards" and "follows company policies." But a new element has been added to include "demonstrates Fredness." Each employee is rated on a four-point scale in regard to their Fred-like qualities (making a positive difference, building relationships, adding value, and reinventing themselves). Cherry Crest has even designed and created a lapel pin to award to employees who score a four in each of the categories.

> **The only thing more powerful than a committed individual is a team of committed individuals.**

Cherry Crest intentionally seeks to hire, develop, and reward Freds. The return on its investment has been irrefutable. The farm receives volumes of positive feedback from customers raving about their farm experience and, in particular, their positive interactions with the "Fredified" staff.

THE ONLY THING BETTER THAN A FRED

One of the big ideas of the Fred principle is that any individual can have a positive impact on others and make a bigger, bolder difference. Few of us, however, work completely alone. We live and interact in family units, organizations, and communities. While our individual actions have an effect, our group efforts have the potential for even greater impact. The only thing more powerful than a committed individual is a team of committed individuals.

But how can you make that happen?

FOUR THINGS EVERY TEAM NEEDS

You don't have to be a team leader to provide these essentials for your team or group.

1. ENCOURAGEMENT

Support your colleagues when you notice their efforts and offer them feedback and encouragement. A kind word can go a long way toward helping others persevere. Support and encouragement can energize a team.

2. EXAMPLES

Look for and describe examples of Fred-like behavior, within and outside your organization. It is better to see a real-life example than to simply discuss an abstract concept. Suggest to your team leader that team members share examples of Fred-like behavior at team meetings. Pick a "Fred story of the week" that best exemplifies what you're trying to accomplish in your organization.

3. IDEAS

Share techniques that have worked in your situation. Regularly ask others, "What is working for you?" Explain what you've tried, what has worked, what hasn't worked, and what you'd do differently next time. Be intentional about communicating ideas and implementation strategies.

4. RECOGNITION

The familiar adage holds true: you get more of what you reward and less of what you ignore.

Anthony Mullins uses the Fred principles in his work in the service industry. He believes in the power of teaching and recognizing Fred-like work. Here's what he does:

> A couple of years ago I implemented a Fred recognition program at the country clubs I managed. We created Fred identification cards and left them around the clubs for our members and guests to recognize the Freds in our company.
>
> We also sent letters to all our members introducing them to Fred and our new employee recognition program. We identified monthly, quarterly, and annual Fred award winners through e-mail blasts, signage, and electronic newsletters. The clubs offered a wide variety of gifts to the Fred winners. It was amazing to see the way everyone embraced the program.

You don't have to be a team leader to recognize the good work others do. Make it a point to reinforce both the attempts and the successes of others on your team who are doing extraordinary things.

HOW TO BUILD A TEAM OF FREDS

1. HIRE FOR FREDNESS.

Paul Noris, president and CEO of the Bank of Central Florida, says that when his company has an opening, the team looks for applicants who tend to enjoy being of service—who have a heart to serve. He believes the bank's ability to provide a high level of client service starts with a willing employee who sees service as the core of his or her being. And as we discussed in chapter 3, Paul sees the Fred philosophy as not limited to customer service but as "a way to lead your life, whether professional or personal."

2. THEME THE TEAM.

Cae Swanger, the CIO for a division of HCA, a national health care company, leads a team of 120 people. She first learned about the Fred idea from a relative and liked the message so much she shared it with her colleagues.

Her company decided to make Fred the theme of their upcoming leadership team conference. Cae described the conference this way:

> We had a wonderful time during the event, enjoying two skits and two presentations, including "A Flight to Fred-ville," complete with an in-flight magazine with Fred puzzles and Fred snacks, a welcome message from the mayor of Fred-ville, and binoculars to help with Fred sightings.
>
> The conference also included ways to enhance our new-hire interview process with Fred-type

questions. Employee badge attachments and office posters reminded us of daily Fred-isms, like May I Monday ("May I help you this week?"), Try It Tuesday (implement a Fred idea), Who's Your Freddy Wednesday (identify a Fred), Thankful Thursday (thank someone today), and Freddy Friday (be a Fred to someone today).

It culminated in a full-feature video demonstrating how *not* to be a Fred, in contrast with the ideal ways to serve our customers. The leadership team then decided we needed to cascade this concept to the entire team, and our final meeting of the year was dedicated to a combined one-hour session of the four presentations. To top things off, our employee advisory group took ownership of establishing a quarterly Be a Fred contest.

Using a theme not only focuses the attention of your team, but it also creates a fun, celebratory atmosphere, which is a big part of what the Fred philosophy is all about.

3. FREDUCATE EVERYONE.

Suncoast Coffee Service and Vending is a small company of twenty employees based in Tampa, Florida. I first learned of them when I received a certificate acknowledging that *The Fred Factor* had been used in their Making People Better office reading program.

The founders of the company, Robert Kantor and Jason Sluka, met in second grade. In 2002 they joined forces and founded a company that delivered fresh smoothie drinks to schools, hospitals, and other local businesses. From there, they added vending items to their product offerings, and later coffee service, break-room items, and janitorial supplies. They run their business according to this mission statement:

> Our mission at Suncoast Coffee Service and Vending is to make our employees, customers, and vendors HAPPY. We successfully create happiness by providing world-class service and products through love, honesty, and integrity, with an overall commitment to excellence for everything we do.

The company's reading program is a prime example of their commitment to "Freducation." Here's how it works: the Making People Better committee makes a book selection based on a theme from one of the owners that focuses on family and business. The books are distributed to employees, along with a "read by" date. Employees have approximately one month to read the book, and they are given fifty dollars after completing it.

The company orders extra copies for customers, and those who receive the book get a personalized letter tied with a green ribbon. Then they send the author of the book a letter and a certificate like the one I received.

At the end of the month, employees meet to discuss the book. They answer questions and highlight points that are of interest to them. Reading the books together promotes a common bond among the employees, whether they're the warehouse manager, a line cook in the café, a route manager, or a director. The endeavor encourages the exchange of ideas and creative thinking, and it acknowledges everyone's thoughts and experience.

There is power in reading good books and sharing ideas as

a team. People tend to learn more (and implement more) when they are engaged in educational opportunities together.

4. DEAL WITH DERFS.

While I was visiting a bookstore that had embraced and sold *The Fred Factor*, one of the employees, Maria, asked me, "Do you know what the opposite of a Fred is?"

I wasn't quite sure what she meant. I knew what the opposite of Fred-like behavior looks like, but I'd never put a name to it before.

"The opposite of a Fred is a Derf!" Maria said. "That's *Fred* spelled backward."

She had a point. Over the years I'd heard about and personally encountered a number of anti-Fred people and organizations. Just recently I had a reader write and say that she works at a company that "sucks the Fredness right out of you!"

Instead of implementing the Fred Factor, some people practice the Derf Factor. Derf principles look something like this:

- Nobody can make any real difference, so why try?
- Relationships are messy; it's better to be left alone.
- It's possible to do things the easy way, with the least amount of effort.
- Each day it's just the same old, same old.

It sounds almost funny to spell out such negative mindsets. What keeps it from being comedic, though, is that we all know people who live by those principles. They might not verbalize it, but their behavior suggests their belief—conscious or unconscious—in the Derf philosophy.

I don't know of anybody who wants to be a Derf. The alternative—being a Fred—is much more enjoyable, not just for everyone around you but also for you personally.

So what's the best way to deal with Derfs?

The first strategy is to use positive peer pressure. When you recognize and reward others for doing the right thing, they'll become less tolerant of those who intentionally or inadvertently undo their good work.

Another strategy is to give constructive feedback. With gentleness but directness, let the person know how he or she is perceived and why. People can't change what they don't understand.

If you are a team leader, you might find yourself in a worst-case scenario—needing to discipline or remove someone from your team **The opposite of a Fred is a Derf. That's *Fred* spelled backward.** who is consistently sowing discord. This isn't just about Fred principles; it's about good team management. You can't discipline someone for "not being a Fred." But discipline might be necessary if an employee is demonstrating disruptive behavior, delivering substandard customer service, or failing to meet other benchmarks.

SHARE FRED OUTSIDE YOUR TEAM

Few have embraced the spirit of Fred as enthusiastically as Don Hartmann, a financial adviser and philanthropic planner. After hearing me speak at our church in Highlands Ranch, Colorado, several years ago, Don bought *The Fred Factor* and read it that day.

Don has done much to spread the message of Fred and has built an extended team of Freds at his business. One of the ways he helped make the Fred philosophy part of his corporate culture was by creating a column in his firm's monthly newsletter about the Freds he encountered.

He called the column "The Fred of the Month," and it immediately became the most popular column in the newsletter. Whenever he saw a colleague or client pick up the latest issue of the newsletter, Don smiled, noticing that without fail they turned to page 3 and read the Fred column before looking at anything else in the newsletter.

Don began to look for more Freds in his daily activities. Whenever he encountered people with Fred-like characteristics, he would tell them he thought they were Freds and explain what that meant. If these were people he worked with on a regular basis, he would give them a copy of the book.

Don even compiled the Fred stories he'd written into a book called *What Fills Your Glass*. Don's column and book spread the message of Fred and helped create a team of Freds within his organization and beyond.

Don explained, "In the vast majority of cases, whenever I mention to someone that I think they're a Fred, they go out of their way to be an even better Fred the next time I need their help with something." He learned that recognizing and encouraging others brings out the best in his team.

At Don's office, there is always a copy of *The Fred Factor* sitting on the coffee table in the reception area. Whenever people pick up the book and start to read it, they are invited to take it with them so they can finish the whole thing.

Don shared, "Many people have told me that they shared

the book with their children, too, because they hoped it would inspire them to become Freds too."

Whether it's through a column in a newsletter, a company-wide reading program, or a Fred-themed leadership conference, recognizing and promoting Fred ideals can transform your workplace into a team of Freds—a united group of committed individuals.

An environment filled with Freds will be much more satisfying and enjoyable than working with nay-saying Derfs. But more than that, a team of Freds will be more effective in providing service to your customers. In other words, creating and being part of a Team Fred is not just good for morale; it's good for your bottom line.

REFLECTIONS FOR LEADERS

1. What Fred-like behavior do you need to specifically acknowledge on your team?

2. What Derf-like behavior do you need to address on your team?

CHAPTER 13

RAISE A FRED JR.

The mediocre teacher tells, the good teacher explains, the superior teacher demonstrates, the great teacher inspires.
WILLIAM ARTHUR WARD

How DOES A MIDDLE SCHOOL get students to turn in $5, $10, or $20 bills found lying on the floor of the hallway, classroom, cafeteria, or auditorium? How do administrators persuade students to come into the office and tell them about the kind comments and actions of their peers? And how do they entice students to respect not only their teachers but their substitute teachers as well?

According to Karen Bayer, the principal at Mackenzie Middle School in Lubbock, Texas, the answer is simple. "The campus reads *The Fred Factor* during breakfast each morning with their advisory groups," she said, "and before you know it, Freds start popping up everywhere!"

I met Karen and members of her team when I spoke to the Lubbock Independent School District Summer Leadership Institute. Karen has a contagious enthusiasm for education in general and for her students most of all.

When I learned about how she and the teachers used *The Fred Factor* at their middle school, I asked Karen about the results they experienced. Here are two of the half dozen snapshots she shared about how students have been affected by the Fred philosophy.

Male student, eighth grade:
Before Fred: The student was kicked out of multiple classes due to poor behavior. He was angry, disrespectful, and truant, and he often got involved in fights.

After Fred: The same student was chosen to be an office aide for one of his forty-five-minute electives, giving him the opportunity to assist students, teachers, parents, and guests each day. Today he has regular attendance, is polite, and has turned around his poor behavior.

Female student, sixth grade:
Before Fred: This student had poor grades, constantly bickered with teachers and peers, was physically aggressive, and was prone to screaming and tantrums.

After Fred: The student's behavior improved, and she started working toward becoming a friend to her peers. She says, "Yes, ma'am" and "Yes, sir" without prompting and has achieved top grades on her report card and district assessments.

I know full well that *The Fred Factor* wasn't solely responsible for the turnaround in these students' behavior. The dedication and skill of Karen and her team enabled the students to take advantage of what they learned, and the book was simply a part of a larger educational experience. But I wanted to know, given her enthusiasm for the Fred philosophy, what role Karen thought *The Fred Factor* played in the creation of Fred Juniors and in the students' improved behavior, grades, and attitudes. Here is how she explained it to me:

> A couple of years ago, I was hired to assist a low-performing middle school filled with extremely angry students and teachers. With improved student performance as our goal, I began teaching and modeling one of the three new *R*s in education: *relationships*.
>
> Each adult in the building was assigned a dozen students. They were responsible for eating breakfast with and monitoring the grades, attendance, and behavior of the children entrusted to their care on a daily basis.
>
> Within a short period of time, these small groups became *family*! I provided many tools to assist them in becoming better acquainted and searched my personal library for a way to help them enjoy some much-needed success. It took only a second to realize that *The Fred Factor* was the perfect tool to assist me in working with these groups. I knew that if Fred's attitude and behavior could be taught and emulated, our campus would be transformed.
>
> And Fred didn't disappoint!
>
> The students loved reading small portions of the book during breakfast each morning. As the text

encouraged them to do, they started looking for Freds on our campus. Pretty soon Fred awards and "Got Fred?" T-shirts were created and issued to extraordinary students and staff members who displayed Fred-like attributes. Students and faculty began looking for the good in one another and relished the positive press.

Thanks to Fred, they experienced some long-awaited behavioral success, and I trust this success will lead to mastery of the remaining two *R*s in education: *relevance* and *rigor*! With all three in place, the goal of improved student performance will be assured.

BETTER SOONER THAN LATER

The only thing better than adult Freds is when kids learn and use the principles.

Wherever you are on your Fred journey, by now you know that the Fred way—making a difference, building relationships, creating value for others, and reinventing yourself—is not just an approach to work but also an approach to life. That's why the Fred values are just as important for kids as they are for adults.

The only thing better than adult Freds is when kids learn and use the principles.

One-fourth of high school students in the United States drop out of school. That's a horrifying statistic in itself, but what happens to those who stay in school? For many young people, the old saying holds painfully true: "Too soon old and too late smart."

Life skills are important at any age, but the tragedy is that some teens develop bad habits in their youth and never manage to master these skills as adults.

One of my mentors, Dr. Earl Kantner, spent twenty-one years at the Ohio Department of Education developing young people. He said, "My goal was to develop them to better quality than they ever thought they could be, and by golly, they achieved that. They were just tickled—they never knew they could be that type of individual, so you can imagine how inspiring that was for them."

Teaching kids—or anyone—the Fred principles is about helping them become better than even they thought they could be.

FRED KIDS

Parents and educators frequently remind me about the importance of teaching the Fred principles to children. The only thing better than learning these lessons as an adult is learning them as a child. The sooner someone understands these timeless truths, the sooner they'll start experiencing the benefits, and the sooner they'll start developing healthy, lifelong habits. Proverbs 22:6 puts it this way: "Train up a child in the way he should go: and when he is old, he will not depart from it."

I was fortunate to have good teachers who instilled in me a love for learning. In high school I did a combined vocational education and college prep curriculum. Since I was a farm kid and had gotten my start in speaking in 4-H, I wanted to belong to the Future Farmers of America (now FFA).

Without a doubt, the most important skills I learned in high school were gained through my participation in FFA. The college prep coursework was necessary for my future success in school, but FFA taught me skills like teamwork, parliamentary procedure, leadership, public speaking, and service. Although at the time I didn't have all the terminology for what I was learning, I was taking in principles that would serve me for the rest of my life.

Whether they learn these lessons at home, in school, or in extracurricular activities, kids need to know that they can make a difference. They need to know that education isn't a preparation for life—education *is* life. Students need to learn how to build healthy relationships and use their creativity to build value for themselves, for their family and friends, and eventually for an employer. Young people also need to realize that each day is a chance to try again—to be better than the day before.

MODEL FRED'S VALUES

Jerry Borne is a technician at Safelite AutoGlass, where he was nominated for the company's Everyday Heroes program under the criteria of "going the extra mile." His story is told in the words of Lydia Evans, a teacher in New Orleans. Her letter of nomination explains what happened:

> Mr. Borne came to my school to install a new windshield for my car, and I was excited that I didn't have to take a day off from work. When he came into my classroom after installing the windshield, I was handling a problem with my students. Someone had taken a child's piece of king cake off his desk and eaten it when the other student was in the bathroom.

We were discussing honesty and how it makes you a better person if you're honest after doing something wrong.

I asked Mr. Borne what would happen if he were dishonest at his job. He talked to my students about doing the correct thing in school and in everyday life. Despite our talk, the student didn't confess.

A few hours later, Mr. Borne delivered a king cake to my school because he felt so bad for the child who hadn't gotten a piece of king cake that afternoon. I was touched that he would go out of his way to make one of my students happy. When he dropped off the cake in the front office, he told the secretary that he has children and would feel awful if that happened to one of his own children.

Another example of someone who models Fred principles to children is my friend Art Holst, a legendary NFL referee. He is now ninety years old, but that doesn't stop him from making a difference. As part of the Ann Arbor Rotary Club in Michigan, he mentors fourth graders in reading at a local grade school during the months he's not in Florida.

No matter who you are, you, too, can impart the Fred philosophy to kids. Here are some steps to get you started.

1. TEACH YOUR CHILDREN WELL.

We all have learned many valuable lessons over the course of our lives, but we often forget to share them. So intentionally set aside some time to verbalize your values to your children. Don't assume that anyone, especially kids, will observe and understand the right values automatically. Remember that many other sources, such as marketers and the media, will try to share their values with your kids. Make sure you get their ear first.

2. DON'T STOP WITH YOUR OWN CHILDREN.

Don't limit your influence to your own kids. Like Jerry and Art, you can share the right values with the other kids you encounter. There's no guarantee that they're hearing about those values from anyone else. As the Bible puts it, don't hide your light under a bushel. By sharing the Fred values with kids, you don't just make a difference for them now; you also make a difference for the future.

3. IT ALWAYS STARTS WITH A RELATIONSHIP.

"Students learn as much for a teacher as from a teacher," Stanford professor Linda Darling-Hammond points out. Great education, like great business, always begins with relationship.

Remember, according to the Fred philosophy, everything is based on relationships. It takes time to establish meaningful, positive relationships with the kids in your life, but it's worth the effort. The great genius of Fred Rogers (aka Mr. Rogers) was his ability to make every child feel special and know that he or she had a friend. By showing real care and concern for children as individuals, just as Fred the Postman does for everyone on his mail route, you show them what it means to be a Fred.

Great education, like great business, always begins with relationship.

4. REWARD READING.

Kids can learn so much on their own if they first learn to love to read. This skill will help them understand more about others and themselves. It will enable them to pursue their interests and passions. And it will show them how they can make a difference in their own way. For kids, reading is the "killer app" that will help them pursue and realize their dreams.

My friend Charlie "Tremendous" Jones used to pay his children to read good books and give him book reports. Just as you might give an allowance based on doing chores around the house, why not provide an incentive to encourage your kids to read? You might want to talk about their findings at a family meal, which would accomplish three good things at once: inspiring reading, encouraging thinking, and providing quality family time.

5. START A CONVERSATION.

We spend most of our time talking about grown-up topics—work, politics, gossip, and the weather. As the popular book title by Adele Faber and Elaine Mazlish puts it, it's worth your while to learn to talk to kids in a way that they will want to listen and to listen to them in a way that will encourage them to talk. Kids can't always express themselves as succinctly and eloquently as adults, but their thoughts and feelings are real and important. Getting them to share their honest thoughts takes time and care, but that effort is something they'll appreciate and remember their whole lives.

6. EXPLAIN AND ENGAGE.

Explain each of the four Fred principles to your kids and then ask, "How might you demonstrate these examples at home?

At school?" You might also talk about how everyone makes a difference—the question is what kind. Then ask your children, "How did you make a difference today?"

Keep in mind that lessons are more readily learned if the children come up with their own applications. Help them craft and improve how they'd apply each of the principles.

7. DON'T DUMB IT DOWN, BUT KEEP IT SIMPLE.

Kids are smarter than we give them credit for. They can understand bigger ideas than they can verbalize. Above all, they don't want to be condescended to—they want to feel like they are always growing up. Sure, your style needs to be simple and direct, but you can still talk to them in a way that lets them know you respect them.

8. RECOGNIZE ANY EFFORT.

Kids, like adults, are often reticent to try something new for fear they might fail. That's why initiative and effort, not just success, should be recognized and reinforced.

I know a youth soccer coach who applauds and praises his players when they miss a shot more than when they make one. Why? When they score a goal, they already have their reward. They are elated. When they miss, they are often dejected. But he wants them to know they have still done something valuable— they made an effort. He encourages them to keep it up, because, as he puts it, "If you don't shoot, you will never score."

FRED AT SCHOOL

Professional educators also play a significant role in raising the next generation of Freds.

Kelly Middleton, the associate superintendent of Mason County Schools in Maysville, Kentucky, shared how implementing the Fred principles throughout her school district helps the schools maintain their position as one of the highest performing districts in the state of Kentucky. All four hundred of its employees have been trained in the Fred philosophy, and they work together at becoming better Freds at their respective positions.

> By going into our students' homes, we find out much more about our students and their parents. One student began acting up at the end of the previous year. While on a home visit, the teacher learned that the mother had cancer. Every time the parent had gone for treatments the previous year, the child would act up in school. Armed with this important information, the teacher now allows the child to call his mother from the classroom before and after the hospital treatments. Since that plan was put in place, the child hasn't had any more discipline problems.
>
> In most schools the number one factor is the state test. In our district it's the children.

In education, it should always be first and foremost about the children. Combining excellent instruction with compassion is a powerful way to create lots of Fred Juniors.

Whether we're parents, educators, or simply individuals who care about the next generation, all of us have a role to play in modeling, teaching, and reinforcing the values we want to instill in the future Freds of our world.

CREATING FREDS OF
THE FUTURE

1. If you have children of your own, decide which principles
   you believe are most important and take responsibility for
   teaching and developing them. Start with one concrete way
   you can instill the most important values in your children.
   Will you read a book together? Will you have a weekly
   discussion about Fred-like behavior at dinnertime? Will you
   take your children to breakfast once a month and spend time
   really listening to them?

2. How can you be a role model to children who aren't your
   own? Will you volunteer at a school? Will you sign up to
   coach a youth sports team or help with the young people at
   your church? Are there other ways you can positively
   influence the growth and development of the next
   generation?

CHAPTER 14

CREATE A COMMUNITY OF FREDS

If we are going to survive, we must build
communities of caring and connection.
CECILE ANDREWS

A PRESS RELEASE dated September 19, 2005, displayed the following headline: "Fort Collins Strives to Be the First Fredville, USA." It goes on to explain that "the entire city of Fort Collins is striving to make the ordinary, extraordinary. The city is creating an environment where positive experiences create positive memories. This in turn encourages visitors to return and residents to be proud of their city."

So what inspired a city to commit to becoming a community full of Freds?

In June 2005, I was invited to speak in Fort Collins. The invitation was extended by Cynthia Eichler, the general manager of Foothills Mall. My speech would kick off the beginning of a six-month initiative to "Find Fred" in Fort Collins, the goal of which was to promote business and spread the message of Fred throughout the entire community.

The city leaders recognized that new competition in the area was threatening to drain business away from the merchants of Fort Collins. Cynthia organized a team of community leaders who decided to use *The Fred Factor* to improve service levels, keep existing businesses, attract new businesses, and raise the quality of life for those in Fort Collins.

This program was initiated by Shop Fort Collins First partners, a group that worked to inspire residents to spend money locally when possible. The partners included the Fort Collins Area Chamber of Commerce, the Downtown Business Association, the Convention and Visitors Bureau, the City of Fort Collins, and Foothills Mall.

More than five hundred people attended the opening session, which was held at the Lincoln Center with help from local merchants and businesses. Following my presentation, a lunch-and-learn seminar was on the agenda. Some 250 individuals stayed to learn how to implement the Fred principles at their organizations.

Cynthia explained how the program worked:

Following the initial keynote address in June, we hosted an event each month for five months. Each month focused on one of the Fred principles, and the final program dealt with hiring and developing Freds. We had events like Breakfast with Fred and Tee'd Off with Fred, and we enjoyed "Fred-tinis." In everything we planned, we tried to make it "funner" (which has become one of our favorite words).

In an attempt to reinforce positive behavior and inspire more of the same, we invited the community to nominate individuals who demonstrated Fred-like qualities. We created a small card that people could use to award an organization when they received extraordinary customer service. We did not limit this to retail venues, and we encouraged people to hand them out with abandon! In addition to retailers, I've given awards to a doctor and his staff and an employee at a drive-through window of a fast-food restaurant. I think it's almost more fun to give out these awards than it is to receive them.

We also introduced a website specifically dedicated to the Fred initiative. The site hosted information regarding the program and facilitated the nominations. Individuals who received the cards could log in, and people could also nominate an individual or business directly on the site. At first nominations trickled in, but it didn't take long for the floodgates to open. We could see firsthand that there are many people in Fort Collins who live passionately.

Thanks to Fred, our community now has some common language we can use to encourage one another to continue living passionately. Not only that, but we've set the bar to provide some gold-plated customer service in Fort Collins.

At the culminating event six months later, the city hosted a special evening called "Fred in Fort Collins: Icing on the Cake." All in attendance saw that the spirit of Fred was indeed alive and well. Postman Fred Shea and I made appearances as we celebrated the extraordinary people in the community.

The awards ceremony recognized two categories: individuals and businesses. Three individuals and one business were awarded top prizes that night, and everyone shared in the winners' successes.

At the end of the initiative, community leaders evaluated the results. Sales tax collection was up. That's a hard number that the city tracks monthly, and although it's impossible to specifically link cause and effect, Shop Fort Collins First believed the increase was due in part to the Fred program. And because they continued to use elements of the program in the following months, the leaders felt a positive residual impact the next year.

Since that time, several other communities have inquired about how to run a Fred initiative, including a woman who used to live in Fort Collins and has since relocated to Arizona, where she works with the local chamber of commerce.

Cynthia summed up the event this way:

> One of the cool things about what we did is that it can
> be done inexpensively. We worked with organizations
> that had limited time and limited budgets. It was
> about sharing information and getting creative, not
> about spending lots of money.

SPREAD THE SPIRIT OF FRED

Fort Collins demonstrated that even an entire community can promote and reward the extraordinary. Their initiative proved the point that going the extra mile isn't just the right thing to do; it also provides a competitive advantage. When people can buy similar products and services anywhere, the differentiating advantage comes from relationship, value, and experience—all of which are created by individuals.

There isn't an organized Fred Factor "movement," but there is an organic, growing Fred community. This community consists of those who enjoy the story, embrace the principles, and live by a similar philosophy. Some people have formed social media groups and created *#fred* hashtags on Twitter. Others have shared their stories online and engaged in conversations with me and with other people. Rarely does a week go by that I don't learn of an organization that has created a training program or a recognition system to promote these principles.

Going the extra mile isn't just the right thing to do; it also provides a competitive advantage.

So what can you do to help spread the Fred spirit in your own community? How might you start an initiative to involve others, whether it's a specific group of people, like your church or civic club, or your entire community?

1. TAKE THE LEAD.

Many people in Fort Collins were involved in creating and conducting the Fred initiative, but Cynthia Eichler led the charge. It was her vision that provided the critical spark.

When Cynthia read *The Fred Factor*, she appreciated that anyone—from a frontline employee to someone behind the scenes—can do something to make a positive difference. "The fact that you didn't need to be a CEO to positively affect the community was very appealing," Cynthia said. That's what compelled her to take the first step.

2. IDENTIFY THE OBJECTIVES.

Shop Fort Collins First had a twofold objective: (1) educate people about how their choices make a difference in the community, and (2) elevate the spirit of service and difference making (aka the Fred Factor) in Fort Collins.

Yes, the group wanted to keep revenue in the city rather than have it go to merchants in other communities. But it wasn't just about gaining a competitive advantage. The number one priority was always the good of the community.

Whatever your objectives are, keep in mind that the more specific they are, the easier it will be to get others on board initially and to evaluate success at the end.

3. FIND LIKE-MINDED PEOPLE.

You always can accomplish more by cooperating with others (think Team Fred). With the energy of a group, not only will you have more good ideas, but you'll also be buoyed by your teammates' moral support and encouragement.

"So many wonderful folks jumped on the bandwagon," Cynthia explained, "we pulled off the planning in six weeks! Everyone got behind the purpose, and that created the initial momentum."

4. CREATE INTEREST.

Share Fred's story and explain the benefits, both practical and personal. Use all the media at your disposal to spotlight what you are trying to accomplish.

Merchants in Fort Collins bought into the program because they saw a need (in their case, a need for a competitive advantage) as well as real potential benefits (a way to retain loyal customers). Everyone has limited time, energy, and resources, so people need to see the payoff—not just psychologically and spiritually, but also practically.

5. INVOLVE AS MANY PEOPLE AS YOU CAN.

Shop Fort Collins First consisted of a team of Freds who did an effective job enlisting other people to get involved. Each of the organizations represented went to their customers and partners, spreading the word about meetings, training sessions, and events. The committee literally hit the street, going door-to-door to deliver letters that introduced the "Find Fred" initiative, explained the format of the program, and included an invitation to the kickoff. They also created a website so the program could be accessed virtually.

Come up with creative ways for people to get involved. Try to find roles for them that utilize their interests, skills, and passions.

6. REGULARLY RECOGNIZE AND REWARD AT A COMMUNITY LEVEL.

The awards ceremony that recognized the Freds found in Fort Collins was the culminating event at the end of the program.

"I was pleasantly surprised by how many people liked the initiative, whether a worker at Burger King or a local physician," Cynthia said. "Interest spanned a broad spectrum in our community."

One of the things that stood out to Cynthia at the ceremony was how powerful it could be to say thank you. "Sometimes people do the right thing for years and aren't recognized as they should be. This program gave us a chance to provide needed appreciation."

BE AN EXCEPTIONAL CITIZEN

You may be involved in community affairs already or be so busy in your personal and professional life that you leave city-wide activities to others. But you make an impact not just through direct volunteer involvement but also in how you interact with others in the community you live in. Something

What would it look like if we took the Fred spirit— choosing to be exceptional rather than ordinary—into our communities?

as simple as driving courteously or being friendly at the park can have a powerful cumulative effect when done thoughtfully and consciously by a whole group of people.

As I travel, I'm often struck by how some communities are so uniformly friendly and others seem just as pervasively unfriendly. Sure, there are exceptions to every rule, but by and large, we have a great effect on each other through our demeanor and behavior.

What would it look like if we took the Fred spirit—choosing to be exceptional rather than ordinary—into our communities?

For one thing, as a collective group, we'd pay at least as much attention to what's right as to what's wrong. It is easy to complain (and it's true that problems need to be addressed rather than ignored), but why not focus as much on the good as the negative?

If we saw a problem, we'd try to figure out what we could offer as a partial or total solution rather than simply determining whom to complain to. We'd talk more and attack less. We wouldn't instantly assume that a different point of view was wrong or hateful, but we'd be willing to consider what we might learn from it.

We'd take a stand for what we believed, but we'd also know why we believed it. We'd do the hard work of understanding our own values and commitments so we could explain them to others. We'd balance the individual good against the good of the community.

And finally, we'd be willing to get involved instead of just spending our time griping. We'd actively support the organizations that are doing work we believe is important. We'd invest our time and money, not just our words.

CITIZEN FRED MAKES A DIFFERENCE

Vancouver, British Columbia, experienced a riot in 2011 after their hockey team lost a key game in the Stanley Cup Finals. More than one hundred people were injured in the disturbance, and by the time it was all over, the city had sustained millions of dollars' worth of damage to public and private property.

In the wake of that tragedy, many people criticized the police officers for not doing enough. Leslie Benisz, however, chose to honor the police officers, some of whom had been seriously injured. He placed thank-you cards and notes of appreciation on every police vehicle he came across on his way to and from work and in his spare time whenever he ventured out. Here's Leslie's reflection on the experience:

> I lost count as to how many cards and notes I placed on
> the windshields of police cars, but I think I may have
> given out as many as one thousand. Many police officers

sent me e-mail messages to thank me for expressing
my appreciation. I even gave a few cops hugs (some
of which were captured on a local TV news camera
and in a newspaper photo). What was important to
me was that I was able to put smiles on some police
officers' faces after such violence had tarnished our city's
image. I may never know how many police officers I
encouraged, but I'm sure my notes of gratitude made
a difference in their lives.

Leslie is proof of the difference one Citizen Fred can make.

CITIZEN OF THE WORLD

Ultimately the world is impacted by small communities working together for change. I've found that the most effective use of
the Fred principles is by people who are united by both location
and mission, whether for-profit companies, nonprofit organizations, schools, or neighborhoods. Significant change always
starts with an individual, then spreads to a few other like-
minded people, and then catches on with a community. When
we work together, we create momentum for positive changes in
our workplaces, communities, and ultimately, our world.

I've been meeting with Juwon Melvin for several years,
advising him on how to grow his business. I'm glad to do so
because his business isn't just about making money; it's about
making the world a better place.

It all began one summer in Spain. After a whirlwind experience of running with the bulls in Pamplona, Juwon returned
to his hotel to check his e-mail. He received a message from

a friend who was serving in the peace corps, inviting him to Morocco for a visit. Always up for an adventure, he packed up his bags.

That trip, he says, changed the course of his life.

His time in Morocco brought him face-to-face with the crushing effects of poverty in a developing country. It broke his heart to see so many children begging on the streets, malnourished and essentially left to survive on their own. He wanted to help, but he knew he couldn't possibly help every child who tugged on his shirt.

"I knew that simply giving money wouldn't solve the real problem," he explained. "I had a background in business, and I wanted to use that knowledge to make a sustainable difference for children in need around the world."

Juwon went to Nicaragua just a few months later, and that experience only intensified his desire to make a significant impact in developing countries.

Upon returning home, he met with his friend Aaron Madonna at a local coffee shop. Aaron was telling his friend about having a reaction to a cheap bar of soap he used while abroad. He had to stay inside his home, embarrassed to go outside until his skin cleared up. Not exactly the way he wanted to start his vacation! Meanwhile Juwon was telling his friend about the living conditions he'd seen in Morocco and Nicaragua.

Juwon captured the story this way:

Somewhere along the way, as we swapped stories, the idea for LifeSoap was born. It started with the idea of selling organic soap that caters to people who have sensitive skin. We figured we could give a portion of each purchase to help children in developing countries receive clean water, better health, and a brighter future. At the same time, we would connect our customers to the projects and the children they were supporting by sharing pictures and updates in every soap box.

Armed with adventurous spirits and a few dollars in their pockets, Juwon and Aaron quit their jobs and invested their time, money, and energy into turning this idea into a reality.

In less than a year, with the support of many people, they were able to cosponsor wells and latrines at two schools in San Lorenzo, Nicaragua. With clean water and sanitation facilities, the children would be healthier and better able to focus on school. This would help them break the cycle of poverty and create a brighter future for their families, their community, and eventually their country.

Juwon smiled as he said, "Now when I look in the children's eyes, I see hope and the promise of a better tomorrow."

Juwon and Aaron are working hard to grow the LifeSoap Company. Their short-term vision is to sell more than twenty-five thousand Boxes of Bliss soap. This will raise the funds needed to sponsor clean water and sanitation projects for children at ten schools in Central America, South America, and Africa.

"We have faith that with hard work, persistence, a spirit of service, and a little bit of luck, we can help change the world," Juwon said. "And so can you!"

Citizen Freds like Juwon and Aaron indeed do change our world, but that change rarely starts at a global level. Change begins behind the doors of your own home and office, within the borders of your own community, and spreads from there. Start with the people you look in the eye each day. Before you know it, the world will be at your back door—or at your own counter, in the soap dish.

COFFEE BREAK

Get together for coffee with a like-minded person who lives near you—someone who shares your values and is invested in the community. Talk about small or big ways you might be able to impact your world. Hold each other accountable by meeting regularly and talking about your progress.

CHAPTER 15

BEST ALWAYS

If man does, day by day, the very best he can, he has no need to worry.
WILLIAM GEORGE JORDAN

BEST ALWAYS. That's how I've been signing correspondence and autographing my books for years. I have two reasons for this signature: first, I want to wish the recipient the best of life always. Second, it is my philosophy and commitment to give my best always. When I do anything less, I not only disappoint those who depend on me, but I also disappoint myself.

That doesn't mean that every single thing I do gets the same investment of attention and effort. That would be wasteful and downright impossible. When you know what is important to you in your life and work, you should apportion your talents and efforts so you can give the best you have to those things.

If you've given your best, then you have done your best. And if you've done your best, then you can be assured you are being all you can be. That's a worthwhile aspiration for all of us.

Do It Well. Make It Fun. That is the title of my friend Ron Culberson's book. Sums things up nicely, doesn't it?

When you know what is important to you in your life and work, you should apportion your talents and efforts so you can give the best you have to those things.

People who do just enough to get by, earn a passing grade, or avoid problems don't get that philosophy. Sure, there are times when good enough is good enough, but not nearly as often as some people's work would lead you to believe. And according to the Fred principles, doing a task well and having fun go hand in hand. If an important undertaking is being done well but the person doing the work isn't having fun, the odds are it won't be done as well as it could be. And even if you can figure out a way to produce great work, but simply suffer through it, what's the point?

YARD BY YARD

In 2007 the *Tampa Bay Times* published a story about Eric Wills that got him a great deal of attention. Eric made news for something rather ordinary: he mowed yards. He was in his midthirties and single at the time, and he mowed fifteen lawns every two weeks in the winter and once a week in the summer in the St. Petersburg, Florida, area. The thing that made this task newsworthy was that he did it for free.

Obviously Eric didn't make his living mowing lawns. He was a postal carrier, and he mowed the yards of some of the people on his route. He did it for a simple reason: the people needed help. Due to age or health problems, they couldn't take care of their lawns themselves, so Eric did it. Nobody asked him to. He just saw a need and met it.

"It's just my little way of making a difference," he told the newspaper. "A yard is a reflection of the person who lives there, so why not help them feel better?"

Several years after the article was published, I wondered what ever happened to Eric. Did he still mow yards? Was he still a postal carrier? I decided to track him down and find out.

I discovered that Eric is no longer mowing those yards. Life has changed completely for him: he got married two years ago, and now he and his wife have a blended family with four children. And the post office still is keeping him busy delivering the mail.

In 2011, he decided that his new life and commitments wouldn't allow him to continue to mow those lawns like he used to. But the very day he made the decision, he ran across an unemployed man who was trying to start a lawn service company.

Some of Eric's equipment had been given to him in the first place as a result of the article. "I got some great donations, like a trailer and a riding mower," he said. "The outpouring from the community was wonderful."

So when it was time to move on from his lawn mowing, he decided to "pay it forward." Eric donated his equipment to the new business owner with the agreement that he would take care of the lawns of those who needed the help most.

While Eric stopped mowing lawns, he didn't stop serving.

"I still serve the same God, but he has given me different marching orders," Eric explained. "My wife and I have gotten involved with a local ministry called Taking It to the Streets, helping out with their food pantry. So I've had a change in direction, but I'm still serving people, doing what I can to help out."

Why does he do it?

"I get involved in anything I see making a difference because I like to see lives get changed," he said.

For Eric, doing his best for others has taken several different forms, depending on what season of life he's in. The key is that he's always involved in giving of himself in some way.

SIX KEYS TO DOING YOUR BEST

Once we've made a commitment to do our best, where do we begin? These steps may seem like common sense, but unless we make a conscious effort to implement, it's easy for them to slip through the cracks.

1. SLOW DOWN.

If you're moving too fast, good things will have a hard time catching you. Don't confuse being reflective with being lazy. Life is about what you accomplish, not just the speed at which you move. Going 100 mph with your hair on fire creates a brief blaze of light but little else.

Rush and hurry are the norms of contemporary culture, yet they are the enemies of the extraordinary. Slowing down may require eliminating a few things of lesser value to establish the space you need to create and connect. Clearing the clutter of busyness can give you the room you need to do your best at what's important.

2. GET OUT.

Opportunity will rarely come to your door. You need to get out of your office and your home and go out into the world. Don't cocoon yourself; instead, put yourself in places of possibility.

Ken Sousa is an associate professor of computer information systems at the collegiate level. A longtime believer in the Fred philosophy, he also believes in the power of getting outside your office.

Ken chaperoned a group of students who participated in a regional competition of SIFE (Students in Free Enterprise) in New York City. During the awards ceremony, Ken found an available seat at a table with some of the students, none of whom he knew personally.

After a few minutes of talking with the young man seated next to him, Ken learned that this student was experiencing some difficulty with Microsoft Excel and had not performed well on his exam. He was stressed about the retest. Sensing his frustration and anxiety, Ken offered to tutor him.

The following Saturday, Ken spent several hours coaching the student in Excel. A week later, the student was excited to tell Ken that he had converted a poor grade into one of the highest scores on the reexamination.

That summer Ken stayed at a resort in Cape Cod that the student had recommended to him. During his stay, he met the student's parents and chatted with them over lunch. They were appreciative of his positive influence on their son.

Since that time, the student has become a committed campus leader. As a sophomore, he is building a résumé of activities, leadership skills, and competitive business experience. The student continues to ask Ken for advice and keeps him up-to-date on how he's doing.

Little efforts can create big ripples. Getting out and engaging people, whether customers, colleagues, or students, is essential to being the best Fred you can be. The results can be life changing, as they were for this student.

3. PAY ATTENTION.

We learn more when we start noticing more. Some opportunities are in plain sight, others are less evident, and a few may be hidden. All will be missed if we're preoccupied or not taking note.

As you go through your day, keep your eyes open to what's happening at a deeper level. What opportunities do you see? What injustices need to be addressed? What problems need to be solved? Who is in need of help that you can provide?

4. DO SOMETHING.

Don't be a spectator in the game of life. The culmination of slowing down, getting out, and paying attention is action—thoughtful, informed action.

When people are seeking my advice, they often ask, "What should I do?" The best answer is that they should do something—anything—as long as it is constructive. Big oaks grow from little acorns, and activity is a precursor to accomplishment. You don't think yourself into success. Thinking is the starting line, but action depends on the driver.

5. ENJOY LIFE.

USA Today reported in a reader poll that 19 percent of respondents couldn't remember the last time they'd had fun.

On the surface it seems odd, if not downright tragic, that we sometimes need to remind ourselves to enjoy our lives. And there are days (or weeks or months) when we think, *Easy for you to say, but I don't have much to enjoy.*

We enjoy life no more and no less than we choose. That's because joy ultimately is a choice. Sometimes we enjoy life more by making the most of a bad situation, and sometimes we enjoy life more by making the most of a good situation. Most of the time, our choice lies somewhere in between.

Enjoyment increases when you make it a point to remember more of the good things. Too often we check off our blessings like they're items on a spiritual to-do list: been blessed, check; had a sacred moment, check. You get the point.

On the flip side, you can enjoy more if you forget more of the negatives in life. I have a bad memory, and that can be a blessing when it comes to the negative things in my past. I'm not living in denial; I acknowledge the imperfections, mistakes, setbacks, and tragedies. I just try to grieve appropriately and then forget about them. Why rehash the bad?

Finally, we can enjoy life more if we forgive quickly. It's a fact of life that people sometimes do us wrong, and life can be unfair. We can't do much about other people or about our circumstances, but we can do something about what and how quickly we forgive, let go, and move on.

6. GET BETTER.

Everyone likes better: better relationships, better health, better jobs, better everything. Have you ever heard anyone say, "Please, don't make it better"? Of course not, because *better* is always an improvement. It increases value. It defeats complacency. It moves us forward.

Customers want *better* too. They like it when they get more in the way of services and benefits, especially when they don't have to pay more to enjoy them.

Better is the most important step to becoming your best. If you want to be your best, you need to start by getting better. Start *doing* better. Good, better, best. That's how it works.

Sometimes we get better quickly in a big way, but that's not how it usually works. More often than not, getting better comes in small, steady increments. Lots of little things done better over time create big improvements.

Is your goal to be 200 percent better? Good luck. Go ahead and try, but you're fighting tough odds. A more realistic goal would be to improve 5 percent each week for the next twenty weeks.

To get better, ask better questions. Here's the first: What is *better*?

Define the improvement. Quantify what it looks like to be better. You can't hit a target you can't see. And remember that different and better aren't always the same. As the expression goes, "All progress is change, but not all change is progress." How do you want to improve? What do you want to become?

Also ask your customer or client what *better* looks like. Most of us have had an idea at some point that we thought was brilliant but the customer thought was, well, not so good. Be sure you understand what *better* is before you start pursuing it.

Then you're ready for the next question: What would make me better?

Ask yourself, and ask others as well—coworkers, colleagues,

your boss, family members. Just make sure they're people who know you well and care enough about you to tell you the truth.

Some people will dodge the question or blow smoke in an effort not to offend you.

If you don't really want to know, don't ask. But if you're truly committed to improving yourself, don't be afraid to be vulnerable with those who are willing to give you some honest suggestions.

Having too many priorities isn't much better than no priorities at all. Pick just one thing you can do better today.

Finally, ask yourself this question, limiting your answer to just one word: What will I do better today?

Consider that not everything needs to be improved. You can only submit accurate expense reports. If they're done neatly and on time, there isn't much room for doing them better.

Having too many priorities isn't much better than no priorities at all. Pick just one thing you can do better today. Not three or four. You'll have a better day . . . and a better life.

THE THREE LOVES

In order to do and be your best, you need three kinds of love.

1. LOVE WHAT YOU DO.

That doesn't mean you love every single moment of every day, but it does mean that at the end of the day you realize you're doing work that is important and beneficial.

And here's a secret: if you really love what you do, you actually love it even when it is hard. I've been to many retirement parties, and I have yet to hear someone say, "You know what I loved about my job? How easy it was. I remember all the easy things we did every day." Instead, I hear people talk with pride about the challenges they met, the setbacks they overcame, and the adversities they tackled. They loved the hard parts because that was where the reward was found.

2. LOVE THE PEOPLE YOU SERVE WITH.

Next to your family, you probably spend more of your life with your coworkers and colleagues than anyone else. Loving them is a key to a rewarding career. The good news is that you don't necessarily have to *like* them. Love is a higher calling, a deeper value. At work, the basis of love is a shared commitment to striving toward a common purpose, serving customers, and making a positive difference. Life is too short to work with people you find impossible to love. Make the choice to love.

3. LOVE THE PEOPLE YOU SERVE.

Customers vote with their time and money. People could get their needs met at any number of businesses or organizations, but they've chosen yours. They've given you their trust and their money. That transaction is so valuable, but it's often taken for granted. We should honor that trust by reciprocating with a love born out of appreciation.

If you can have all three of these loves, you truly are blessed. Loving what you do, the people you serve with, and the people you serve sets the stage for you to do and be your best always.

And if you have these three loves, I can assure you that you are a Fred.

Ralph Waldo Emerson said, "Make the most of yourself, for that is all there is of you." Doing your best in whatever you do will make you the best you can be. What we do, especially for others, defines the impact of our lives. It's all we have to offer. Make it better. Make it *the best*.

Afterword

CINDY SHULTZ lives in a small town in the Midwest. Every Sunday her parents, Darwin and Ellen, who are in their late seventies, attend a small country church a few miles from town.

Each week after church, Cindy's dad calls ahead to the local Donatos pizza place with the same order: two individual classic trios. And every Sunday when they pick up their order, they are greeted by a small-in-stature gentleman named Eric.

Cindy described Eric this way: "Eric is always smiling and ready with a joke for my dad. When he rings up their order, he inquires about their day and the previous week."

One rainy Sunday, Eric anticipated the couple's arrival and was waiting in the parking lot with an umbrella to help Ellen into the restaurant so she wouldn't get wet. Afterward Darwin couldn't wait to tell Cindy that he had taken a picture on his cell phone and texted it to the Donatos corporate office—a major accomplishment, Cindy said, since her dad is "*not* tech savvy."

One Sunday Eric wasn't there to greet Darwin and Ellen. Disappointed, they inquired about Eric's unusual absence. The young cashier explained, with tears in her eyes, that Eric wasn't feeling well. It was the first time she recalled Eric ever calling off from work. Apparently his arthritis had flared up, and it was too painful for him to walk to work.

Cindy learned that Eric was a veteran and suffering from debilitating arthritis. The VA covered his medical expenses, but with his disability, Eric didn't drive or own a car. He walked to work, rain or shine, and lived alone in a room at a nearby boardinghouse.

Cindy's dad worried about Eric all week and was relieved to see him back at work the following Sunday. Cindy began to suspect that while her dad would never admit it, the pizza wasn't her parents' biggest motivation for driving into town. It was his bond of friendship with that employee—not only a fellow veteran but also a true Fred.

One particularly hot Sunday in May, Cindy's mom invited her to ride to town with them for a late lunch at Donatos. Eric was off the clock but was still at the restaurant. After exchanging greetings and jokes with Darwin, Eric sat at an empty booth reading a book and occasionally helping out the new girl at the register.

As they were leaving, Darwin discovered that Eric still was at the restaurant because his fan was broken at the boardinghouse. He was planning to stay at work until it cooled off.

After a quick trip to the store, Darwin delivered the new fan to Eric, who was still sitting in the booth.

"Stay cool," he said to a surprised Eric.

"Wow!" Eric looked utterly surprised. "Thanks!"

Cindy shared, "They didn't talk long, but I saw enough of their exchange to understand what it meant. Two people were friends who otherwise would have been strangers, had it not been for this man who was a Fred. They were two veterans who looked out for each other, as it should be."

Life isn't always easy. But some things in life are simple—like taking care of each other. The essence of the Fred principle is exactly that: individuals who choose to be of service to another. It might not be part of their job, but it is always part of their philosophy. And even though those acts of service aren't done with expectation of reciprocity, the kindness is often returned.

Albert Einstein was known as one of the world's greatest scientific minds and a groundbreaking theoretical physicist, but I've often marveled at his wisdom about human nature. He said, "We know from daily life that we exist for other people first of all, for whose smiles and well-being our own happiness depends." I think that's what the apostle Paul was talking about when he said, "Serve one another humbly in love" (Galatians 5:13, NIV).

These words ring true all these years later in our own experiences . . . and in the experience of two veterans in a small Midwestern town. One enjoys a pizza with his wife after church, and the other helps provide it—and stays cool with appreciation. As they enrich each other's lives, they demonstrate in simple yet significant ways that we exist for others.

As it should be.

Acknowledgments

To Matt Yates and Sealy Yates, my literary agents at Yates & Yates, for their representation and friendship. This is our fifth book together!

To Stephanie Rische, my cheerful and supportive editor, who always makes my writing better.

To Jon Farrar, Ron Beers, April Kimura-Anderson, and the many other team members at Tyndale who help and support me in so many ways (including laughing at my bizarre sense of humor).

To all of those who not only read *The Fred Factor* but lived it and became the stories I shared in this book, including Michael Flowers, Tom Peters, Richard Robinson, Dr. Matt Messina, Jim Hunsicker, Mae Wiggins, Edgar Ramirez, Jim and Naomi Rhode, Stephanie Ponti, Jennifer Griffith, Kevin King, Taylor Scott, Jim Morris, Court Durkalski, Brian Waltman, Anthony Mullins, Robert Kantor, Paul Noris, Jason Sluka, Cae Swanger, Don Hartmann, Karen Bayer, Dr. Earl Kantner, Jerry Borne,

Lydia Evans, Art Holst, Kelly Middleton, Cynthia Eichler, Leslie Benisz, Aaron Madonna, Juwon Melvin, Eric Wills, Ken Sousa, and Cindy Shultz. I appreciate you all!

To Fred and Kathie Shea, for their continued support of my work and their input for this book.

To my team at Sanborn & Associates Inc.—Dannielle Thompson and Helen Broder. Thanks for keeping me "on the road" with my message.

To my parents, Dorothy and Leslie Sanborn, for teaching me how to be a Fred before I even knew what it meant.

To my family—my beautiful wife, Darla, for her wisdom and love, and my sons, Hunter and Jackson—for bringing so much joy into my life.

And, as always, I acknowledge my Creator. I am greatly favored and deeply blessed.

About the Author

Mark Sanborn is the president of Sanborn & Associates Inc., an idea lab for leadership development. Leadershipgurus.net lists Mark as one of the top-thirty leadership experts in the world.

In addition to his experience leading at the local and national levels, he has written or coauthored eight books and is the author of more than two dozen videos and audio training programs on leadership, change, teamwork, and customer service. He has presented more than two thousand speeches and seminars in every state and in a dozen countries.

Mark is a member of the prestigious Speakers Roundtable, which represents the top speakers in the world today. Mark holds the title Certified Speaking Professional (CSP) from the National Speakers Association and is a member of the CPAE Speaker Hall of Fame.

Mark's book *The Fred Factor: How Passion in Your Work and Life Can Turn the Ordinary into the Extraordinary* is an international bestseller and was on the *New York Times, BusinessWeek,* and *Wall Street Journal* bestseller lists. His latest books include *You Don't Need a Title to Be a Leader: How Anyone, Anywhere, Can Make a Positive Difference; The Encore Effect: How to*

Achieve Remarkable Performance in Anything You Do; and *Up, Down, or Sideways: How to Succeed When Times Are Good, Bad, or In Between.*

Mark is a past president of the National Speakers Association and winner of the Cavett Award, the highest honor bestowed by that organization. In 2007 Mark was awarded the Ambassador of Free Enterprise Award by Sales & Marketing Executives International.

He lives in Highlands Ranch, Colorado, with his wife, Darla, and sons, Hunter and Jackson.

Twitter: @mark_sanborn
Facebook: marksanbornspeaker
Blog: www.marksanborn.com/blog

Learn more about how to deliver extraordinary results with *Fred 2.0*.

Begin with a Free *Fred 2.0* Webinar and Other Resources

Continue to learn about the ideas discussed in this book. We've made the next step as simple and inexpensive as possible—it's free! Visit www.marksanborn.com/fred2 to take advantage of these learning resources: a webinar, a summary handout of the key principles in this book, and a subscription to *Leadership Lessons*, Mark's e-zine.

Order Learning Resources Today

Mark has created many learning resources, including books, CDs, DVDs, and DVD-based training programs. Learn more about how you and your team can benefit from these resources by visiting www.marksanborn.com/store.

To learn more about live programs for your organization, visit www.marksanborn.com or call 303-683-0714.

Bring Mark Sanborn to Your Organization

Mark Sanborn is an award-winning speaker known for his entertaining and educational presentation style. He provides audiences with actionable ideas and powerful insights on leadership, customer service, and motivation. Having Mark speak can make your next meeting or event extraordinary.

To bring Mark Sanborn to your organization, visit www.marksanborn.com or call 303-683-0714.